THE
Capsule Wardrobe

1,000 OUTFITS FROM 30 PIECES

Wendy Mak

SKYHORSE PUBLISHING

Skyhorse Publishing books may be purchased in bulk at special discounts
for sales promotion, corporate gifts, fund-raising, or educational purposes.
Special editions can also be created to specifications. For details, contact
the Special Sales Department, Skyhorse Publishing, 307 West 36th Street,
11th Floor, New York, NY 10018 or info@skyhorsepublishing.com.

Skyhorse® and Skyhorse Publishing® are registered trademarks
of Skyhorse Publishing, Inc.®, a Delaware corporation.

Visit our website at www.skyhorsepublishing.com.

10 9 8 7 6 5 4

Library of Congress Cataloging-in-Publication Data is available on file.

Cover design by Laura Klynstra

Print ISBN: 978-1-5107-1349-9
Ebook ISBN: 978-1-5107-1351-2

Printed in China

Table of Contents

Acknowledgments

Firstly, to all the baubles, bling, and glitz in my wardrobe that I have owned, loved, and worn over the years while I discovered my style.

Next, to all the brands, labels, and retailers—from the well-known to the undiscovered—that have inspired the pieces you see here today in *The Capsule Wardrobe*!

Last, but not least, to my husband, my family and friends, and the loves of my life—my bulldogs, Dora and Iggy, and my cat, Sparkles—who have made looking stylish while having fur on my dress a daily challenge I relish (and wouldn't have any other way).

INTRODUCING

The Capsule Wardrobe

> "WOMEN USUALLY LOVE WHAT THEY BUY, YET HATE
> TWO-THIRDS OF WHAT IS IN THEIR CLOSETS."
> —MIGNON MCLAUGHLIN

If Mignon McLaughlin's quote resonates, then welcome—this book is for you!

As a professional stylist, I've seen firsthand the angst some women go through when it comes to the daily task of dressing and shopping. In fact, it probably comes as no surprise to know that (if you add it all up) women can literally spend years of their lives trawling the shops for clothes!

Yes, there are a handful of women out there who genuinely enjoy idly rifling through endless racks of clothes for hours—but the majority I meet would rather be doing something else, like spending time with their loved ones or eating chocolate ice cream while drooling over a young George Clooney in reruns of *ER* instead of being stuck in the shops, tormented by clothes that don't fit or flatter.

Having styled thousands of women of all ages, sizes, and shapes with very real lifestyles, budgets, and bodies, I've also witnessed the emotions involved when it comes to our wardrobes.

You see, it's very rarely just about "the clothes." Our clothes represent us. What we wear makes a statement to the outside world. How we *feel* in what we're wearing can define our moods and emotions for the day.

Because of this, we end up spending a lot of time fussing, worrying, and shopping (and then shopping some more!) to find this nirvana of wardrobe happiness.

And this is where the capsule wardrobe comes into play.

More than just creating hundreds of outfits from a handful of pieces, the capsule wardrobe is about a lifestyle.

The capsule wardrobe lifestyle embraces a minimalist wardrobe—a simpler take on fashion—and how to feel and look good with less.

Dressing every day doesn't have to be a chore. It *can* be simple, easy, and worry-free. If you know what to look for, you'll be able to open up the door to your closet and confidently say, "I know exactly what I am going to wear today, and I love it!"

So, is achieving this kind of wardrobe happiness elusive? Perhaps not as much as you might think.

How? Simple.

Banish the clutter. Simplify your wardrobe.

CLUTTERED CLOSETS CREATE CLUTTERED LIVES

Clutter is an evil.

Please don't misunderstand—I'm not talking about the possessions that make you genuinely happy. I'm talking about the stuff that weighs you down. The kind of stuff that sucks your energy faster than you can say, "Jimmy Choo."

It's clutter in our wardrobes from owning so much, yet consistently having "nothing to wear." It's also clutter in our minds from what we perceive are our bodies' flaws and then overcompensating for this with *more* physical clutter by buying additional clothes.

Take a moment to calculate how much you've bought and either never worn or worn less than a handful of times. You're not alone. Collectively across the globe, this would easily amount to billions of dollars of clothes languishing in closets that will never see the light of day.

A cluttered closet so full you can barely see past the first blouse takes up far too much valuable mental (head) and emotional (heart) space.

Yet, I also acknowledge that, on the other hand, too few items creates angst.

The trick is finding the balance—enough key pieces to form the platform from which you can create classic, everyday outfits, along with enough pieces to add interest, accents, and colors that will keep you looking fashionably up-to-date, season to season.

And this is what the capsule wardrobe is all about.

WHAT IS THE CAPSULE WARDROBE?

In a nutshell, a capsule wardrobe is a mix-and-match wardrobe that creates multiple outfits from just a handful of pieces.

The concept of capsule wardrobes is not new, but in my particular capsule wardrobe I'll show you the exact thirty styles and pieces that can be worn in over one thousand different ways to suit the majority of occasions in your life.

This isn't another predictable and fluffy "10 Basics Every Woman Should Own" article that has been reproduced more times than Brad and Angelina have adopted children, but a realistic list of thirty actual pieces you can wear and re-wear in so many ways, you'll have an outfit for almost any occasion (except maybe your own fabulous wedding and Halloween).

Collectively, I affectionately refer to these thirty pieces as the "Terrific Thirty!"

Plus, I'll share step-by-step advice on how to review and edit your own wardrobe, as well as the insider stylist secrets I've been using for years to avoid critical fashion mistakes when you next shop.

This book is about identifying versatility and perhaps choosing fewer, but quality, items rather than buying lots of things on impulse or, worse, on a bad day. (I should know—I once came home after a bad breakup with sequined hot pants that no woman's booty, except for maybe J. Lo's, should ever be seen in!)

And while we'd love to think we have endless amounts of money to spend on clothes (gee, fiscal responsibility sucks!), the capsule wardrobe will show you that you don't need to spend mountains of cash on a closet stuffed full of clothes. In fact, it will help extend your budget by miles.

If you choose wisely (and I'll show you how), each item will serve you so well in multiple outfits that you'll be blown away. Maybe as blown away as the first time you read *50 Shades of Grey* . . .

BUT FIRST, LET'S ADDRESS THAT MIND CLUTTER . . .

I'm a firm believer that cluttered closets create cluttered lives and minds.

This *mind clutter*, as I call it, is something we're all guilty of, myself included.

It's the time we spend in our minds, focusing on what's no longer perfect or beautiful about our bodies.

It's the fact that women are so good, almost gifted really, at zeroing in on the bits of our bodies that have gone south that we can't see anything else but what we feel are our saggy boobs, a one-pack tummy, wobbly arms, and puffy ankles!

Here's a simple exercise to show you what I mean. Sit down, grab a sheet of paper, and write down the top three concerns you have about your body. Then write down the three things you love best about your body.

I'll bet that nine out of ten of you were able to list your concerns in a heartbeat, but probably took time to pause and think before writing down what you love best about yourself.

We're so conditioned to looking at the worst aspects of our bodies and what we want to change or wish we still had that we lose sight of what's still good!

The reality is that our bodies are dynamic, evolving, and precious *just as they are right now*! As my oldest, dearest seventy-eight-year-old client, Dot, once said to me, "Wendy, if I realized at fifty how much worse my body would be at seventy, I'd have stopped complaining so much and shown my body off a lot more. And had lots more sex."

After I quietly picked myself up from the floor following dear old Dot's comments about her bedroom antics, I realized that she is right!

We can keep wishing we were still nineteen, twenty-nine, thirty-nine, or forty-nine, or we can love our bodies as they are *today*. We can focus on the past or we can embrace our bodies exactly as they are now—because you only get one body. So if it's healthy and working, then you are **stunningly beautiful**.

HOW TO USE THE CAPSULE WARDROBE

The items in the capsule wardrobe that are detailed over the next few chapters are suggested key staples that will give you a solid foundation from which to create hundreds and hundreds of outfits.

But if you're not a natural born fashionista, don't worry. In the Appendix on page 122, I've mapped out the entire list of one thousand outfit combinations using the thirty capsule wardrobe pieces, so you can simply refer to the list and pick out an outfit!

However, more important than what the actual pieces or outfits are is how you "re-train your brain" to shop like a stylist. Channel your inner stylist to see how a really simple addition or change (for example, swapping in a bag or adding a blazer) can instantly create a whole new look—in seconds.

Also, don't hold back and stick to my list alone. Let your creativity guide you—think about how adding an extra blouse or pair of shoes to your capsule wardrobe might give you even more options to add to your list of outfits!

This isn't about how to dress body shapes or work out your best colors. Nor is this the book for you if you're someone that naturally finds fashion instinctive and revels in experimenting with mountains of clothing.

This is a book about learning how to become the Queen of Capsule Dressing so you can get laser-focused on only buying what you *need* rather than being distracted by desperation shopping.

Also—and this is *muy importante*—while the book outlines thirty recommended basics, this doesn't mean you can't have any more than thirty pieces in your closet. On the contrary! There's never a one-size-fits-all solution. All of us have different body shapes, physical quirks, and personalities that make each of us unique, beautiful, and special.

For that reason, use the capsule wardrobe to help guide your choices, but remember that it's perfectly okay to adapt the list and adjust it (or even add a few extra items) for the weather you live in or to better reflect your lifestyle.

A FEW LAST THINGS . . .

While I don't include jewelry and accessories such as scarves or hats as part of the official list of items in the capsule wardrobe, they are important to help you create your thousand outfits.

As they're hugely personal, accessories are the best way to express your individuality. Your banged-up gold bangles, diamond pendant, feathered old brooch, favorite cocktail ring, and even your grandma's perfect, vintage pearls help tell *your* story so you're able to individualize your thirty pieces and make this wardrobe collection truly your own.

I've also made the assumption that your typical wardrobe will require some work wear (and that your work wear isn't uniform based), weekend wear, and going-out outfits. I've also left out anything you wear to lounge around in at home and gym wear or anything you actively sweat in!

If your lifestyle is a little different, simply swap a couple of the pieces that you won't need for something more suitable (for example, if you don't go anywhere dressy often, remove the high heels for another pair of flats).

That's the beauty about the concept of a capsule wardrobe—nothing's set in stone and you can adapt the elements and pieces to best suit you, your lifestyle, your culture, and the climate.

If you can learn the *art* of mixing and matching, you can apply it to any wardrobe!

And now, let the wardrobe happiness begin.

Happy Styling!

THE GREAT CLOSET
Clean-Out

IT'S NOT ABOUT CLEANING YOUR CLOSETS. IT'S ABOUT CHANGING YOUR LIFE.

If you've ever stared at a full closet and wondered what to wear, you're not alone.

We've *all* been there. Changing outfits six to seven times and feeling unhappy with each of your choices. Reaching into your closet and finding yet another item that you've never worn. Looking at something and wondering, *what do I wear with this?!*

It's a frustrating feeling, and I call it the "Mocking Wardrobe."

It mocks you with its piles and racks of clothes that go unworn every time you open up the closet doors. This wardrobe gives Carrie Bradshaw a run for her money (and, sadly, without Mr. Big's amazing walk-in closet!). It contains so many beautiful pieces, it's literally endless, and yet you still have nothing to wear.

If we're going to overcome the Mocking Wardrobe and find true happiness hanging in the closet, it's going to take some hard work, dedication, and a great, big, no-holding-back closet clean-out!

By embracing the concept of only thirty terrific pieces to create one thousand outfits, you'll kick that Mocking Wardrobe out of the house for good and be on the road to true wardrobe happiness.

A perfect opportunity to simplify your wardrobe *and* your life.

CUT THE CLUTTER

Cutting clutter is the simplest key to wardrobe happiness. We need to dump all excess items or else your new capsule wardrobe will simply get lost in the old jam-packed closet.

In my experience, women are terrible when it comes to "moving on" items in their wardrobe. We tend to get very emotional . . .

"BUT I BOUGHT THAT ITCHY, LACE-FRILLED GYPSY SKIRT WITH THE HOT PINK CROCHET WHEN I WAS IN INDIA ON HOLIDAY FOR MY FORTIETH . . . I CAN'T *POSSIBLY* THROW THAT OUT!"

We might even feel incredibly guilty . . .

"MY HUSBAND BOUGHT ME THAT HANDBAG FOR CHRISTMAS SEVEN YEARS AGO. I CAN'T BRING MYSELF TO THROW IT OUT, EVEN IF IT'S USELESS SINCE IT'S TOO SMALL TO FIT ANYTHING I NEED!"

We justify why we can't move something on . . .

> "I SPENT $280 ON THOSE JEANS AND THAT'S A LOT OF MONEY. I CAN'T THROW THEM OUT EVEN IF MY BUTT LOOKS AS FLAT AS A PANCAKE IN THEM."

We also (and I hate to say it!) can be very unrealistic . . .

> "THOSE MESH PANTS I BOUGHT IN 1987 WERE VERY COOL BACK THEN. SURELY ALL TRENDS COME BACK INTO FASHION AT SOME STAGE?"

> "I'LL HANG ON TO THIS DRESS. IT'LL LOOK GREAT WHEN I START DOING 1,078 SIT-UPS A DAY TO TRIM DOWN MY TUMMY. I'LL JUST SET MY ALARM FOR TWO HOURS EARLIER TO DO THEM!"

Alright, get ready for some tough love.

Ladies, it's time to stop making excuses. Bad fashion mistakes, clothes that aren't "you," things that haven't fit for years, and items that are simply just worn or outdated have no place in your wardrobe. No matter how much money you've spent on them.

Yes, you heard me right. It doesn't matter how much money you've spent on them.

These items take up valuable physical and mental—heart and mind—space in your life. It's simply bad wardrobe karma.

CLUTTERED CLOSETS TAKE UP VALUABLE
PHYSICAL AND MENTAL SPACE.

Free up this space to give yourself room for
your new capsule wardrobe lifestyle.

These clothes clutter your life and, most important, they clutter your *thought process*, making it even harder to decide what to wear.

STEP 1: ZERO EMOTION

The first step in your great wardrobe clean-out is to take charge of your wardrobe clutter and approach it as I would with clients of mine—with zero emotion and no sympathy.

While this sounds harsh, you can't be emotional about this process or nothing will be moved on from your closet.

Try to separate yourself from the guilt, unrealistic promises, and sentimental gushing (you can do it!), and I promise you that in a month's time you won't even remember what you had in it originally.

A simple example is bridesmaid dresses. They take up *so* much room in our closet, but we feel guilty about throwing it out as it is a memento from "so-and-so's wedding," and heaven help us if the bride found out!

15

Here's the thing—every bride lies and says you can wear the bridesmaid's dress again. Let's be honest. You wouldn't be caught dead a second time in that piglet-pink horror.

So, remove the emotion, and, for the love of all the fashion gods above, throw it out. Remember—zero emotion when you're doing your closet clean-out.

STEP 2: MAKE DECISIONS

Now it's time to start the hard part of your clean-out: making tough decisions.

Hard decisions are necessary if you want to cut the clutter. Review all items in your closet and make a decision about *everything*. Leave no pile unturned, and don't hang on to anything simply because you couldn't decide what to do with it.

MAKING DECISIONS

1. Is the item a Keep, Toss, Alter, Give Away, or Sentimental piece?
2. Every item *must* have a "friend" to wear it with.
3. Think outside of the box.
4. Make your wardrobe visually appealing.

To help you make decisions, use the following tools.

1. THE KTAGS SYSTEM

The KTAGS system simply says that every item reviewed *must* fall into one of the following categories:

- KEEP—this is a sure winner. It fits well, it's in good condition, you love it, and it's up-to-date. This can stay in your wardrobe.
- TOSS—this item doesn't work for you anymore and needs to be tossed out as it's too worn or stained to give away.
- ALTER—this can stay, provided it can be easily altered to fit/create an updated look.
- GIVE—this doesn't work for you anymore but is still in great condition or new enough to be given away to a friend or a charity.
- SENTIMENTAL—store anything sentimental such as grandma's cardigan or your wedding dress away from your main closet.

An easy rule of thumb when deciding whether something should be kept or not is to ask yourself how you feel in it when you wear it.

Do you put it on and take it off straight away because you don't feel right in it? Is it the piece that you keep tugging and fiddling with all day because it just doesn't sit comfortably on you?

If it falls into one of those categories, then it's a clear "toss" or "give-away," depending on its condition.

2. EVERY ITEM MUST HAVE A "FRIEND"

This step is one that most people miss when conducting a wardrobe clean-out. If you decide to keep an item, it must have a "friend" to play with in the closet!

A "friend" is something you can wear alongside or match with said item. If it doesn't have a "friend," the item needs to go. The only exception is if you intend to buy something else to match with it.

It's tempting to give this "friend" rule a miss, but if you don't abide by it you'll find that, despite your best efforts, a closet full of random clothes that don't match will still confront you on a daily basis.

3. THINK OUTSIDE OF THE BOX

If you're always grabbing the same skirt to wear with the same top, then it's time to mix it up!

Reach for a different skirt—in a different shape, color, or fabric—or try it with jeans. Do something different!

Pick pieces you wouldn't normally think could go together and try them on. At worst, you're no worse off than before, and at best, you'll be pleasantly surprised and have a whole new outfit without spending a dollar.

4. MAKE YOUR CLOSET VISUALLY APPEALING

Retailers "merchandise" their stores to make them appealing to you visually. When you see clothing laid out in a beautiful, ordered, and logical manner, you're more likely to make a purchase.

The same concept applies to your closet. Your closet is valuable—prime real estate—so first create room and space by doing your clean-out. Then, organize all items logically and you'll be able to see what you own, what you haven't worn in ages, and (most importantly) you'll be able to create new and different outfits with far less effort than if you were fruitlessly rifling through piles of clothes squeezed into a closet.

When you can see all the items you own, you'll finally be able to create new combinations!

I personally like to "merchandise" my wardrobe by creating categories of similar types of clothing.

For example, all jeans sit together, all blouses are hung in the same section, all pants share the same space, all casual tees and tanks are folded as a family, and the same goes for all dresses, skirts, blazers/coats, and so on and so forth. I also like to use the same type of hanger for everything as you can fit a lot more clothes in that way.

Others prefer to order their wardrobe by color, so everything black is placed together, all whites sit in a row, and so on.

Whichever way works best for you, create this order and stick with it!

STEP 3: DON'T FORGET THE ACCESSORIES

As we're often heavily focused on the clothes, we may forget to review and purge our accessories. Here are a couple of tips on de-cluttering accessories.

1. THANKS FOR THE MEMORIES

Accessories can hold a lot of emotion, but if you're hanging on to jewelry that's tarnished or old, it may be time to let go (or put it in your sentimental box).

2. PAINFUL SHOES

They may be sexy, but if you need medical attention for the blisters that form within minutes of wearing them, it's time to let those painful shoes go for good. No amount of fashion is worth that pain (you heard it here first)!

3. IMPRACTICAL BAGS

Even I've fallen victim to buying bags that I've loved but that have not been very practical. A notorious mistake is the "in-betweener" handbag—too big to be a clutch or going-out bag, and yet not big enough to hold my everyday essentials.

Or perhaps it's the bag that doesn't have a secure closure, and you're always worrying about things falling out of it. Whatever the case, these are the bags that should be re-homed to a new owner. Lots of worthy charities would love to receive bags and shoes in great condition.

SUMMING IT UP

Congratulations! You're officially on the road to wardrobe happiness! You have cut the clutter and made decisions that will ultimately lead to the room you need (physically and mentally) for your new capsule wardrobe lifestyle.

Reward yourself with a hot bath and a cup of tea, or a glass of wine, chocolate, and another episode of *The Real Housewives*—because in the next chapter we're going to start planning our capsule wardrobe.

PLANNING: THE KEY TO

Wardrobe Happiness

> "EVERY MINUTE YOU SPEND IN PLANNING SAVES TEN MINUTES IN EXECUTION."
>
> —BRIAN TRACEY

Planning is the key to creating wardrobes that work. It may take you thirty minutes to do now, but it will save you precious time (and money) from fashion mistakes, such as buying the non-essentials.

WHAT KIND OF SHOPPER ARE YOU?

First, we need to understand what kind of shopper you are.

Most of us fall into one of two categories when it comes to our style of shopping. As you build your capsule wardrobe, you need to know what type of shopper you are to avoid repeating any past mistakes.

Let's take a look at the two most common shopping styles, and then you can decide which one describes you best.

SHOPPER #1: BORING BETTY

Boring Betty is, as the name implies, well, a little boring! She is absolutely fantastic when it comes to buying practical (but oh-so-dull) basics.

She stocks up on items such as work clothes effortlessly because, to Boring Betty, it's like buying a uniform—easy to shop for with no thought for new trends, experimenting with color, or attempting a new style.

While Boring Betty usually always finds something to wear, it's likely to be the same style over and over again. This makes her feel quite drab and sometimes even frumpy, because there's nothing very exciting in her humdrum wardrobe full of basics.

SHOPPER #2: SPARKLING SALLY

Sparkling Sally is a fashion icon, at least in her mind. When she hits the shops, like a magpie she's attracted to all of the shiny, interesting pieces that come and go with the seasons.

She loves anything dressy and tends to buy pieces for special occasions. She buys her clothes out of impulse or love, and collects pieces that are more fun than functional.

Unfortunately, this means Sparkling Sally usually has little to wear for everyday situations such as work! She has an endless array of fabulous statement pieces but lacks the daily basics to pair them with.

WHAT KIND OF SHOPPER
ARE YOU?

1. BORING BETTY

Lots of basics like everyday casuals or work clothes.
Falls into the trap of buying the same styles or brands
over and over again.

2. SPARKLING SALLY

Attracted like a magpie to all things shiny and fancy.
Finds shopping for practical items like a plain black
skirt uninspiring.

THE 80/20 RULE

Knowing what kind of shopper you are is crucial, because the secret
to a successful capsule wardrobe is to get a balance of both styles—the
strong foundation of Boring Betty's classic pieces with a good dose of
Sparkling Sally's eye for style.

An easy formula to create this balance is to use the 80/20 Rule.

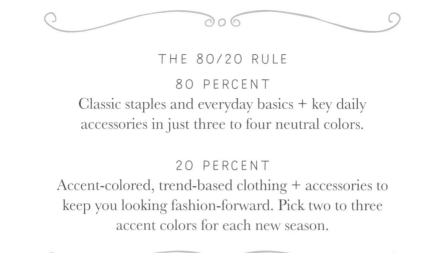

THE 80/20 RULE

80 PERCENT

Classic staples and everyday basics + key daily
accessories in just three to four neutral colors.

20 PERCENT

Accent-colored, trend-based clothing + accessories to
keep you looking fashion-forward. Pick two to three
accent colors for each new season.

Think of the 80/20 rule like a wedding cake. The bulk of it (80 percent) is made of a solid, usually vanilla, base. You need it—it's the foundation of the whole cake—but it's also incredibly boring on its own.

But, add the cream in the middle as well as that gorgeous icing on top and you have yourself a delicious confection that you can't stop looking at! This decadent decoration might only form 20 percent of the actual cake, but it's what makes the cake indulgent and beautiful.

THE 80 PERCENT—FOUNDATIONAL BASICS

This simple rule means that roughly 80 percent of your wardrobe should be staple basics that you can dress up or down easily.

The trick is to look for classic pieces that aren't fussy and that don't have a lot of detail on them, so that they don't date too quickly.

When I work with my clients to create this foundation for their capsule wardrobe, I also get them to choose their 80 percent within just three or four "base" or "neutral" colors. These include colors such as white (or off-white), creams, stone, beige, black, gray, charcoal, navy, brown, and also denim.

If you do this, the majority of your basics and staples will be in neutral colors, which means they'll always match one another in terms of color. You can throw on a pair of trousers and a top, knowing that they'll go together without even needing to look in the mirror.

But I'm the first to admit that wearing gray, black, and white (or whatever your three or four base/neutral color selections are) all the time is incredibly boring!

This is where we need the other 20 percent of your capsule wardrobe.

THE 20 PERCENT—FASHIONABLE ADDITIONS

These are the fun pieces a Sparkling Sally would buy. When worn with Boring Betty's basics, they will change your outfit completely and keep you looking on-trend, contemporary, and modern.

Because these are the fashion pieces in your wardrobe that are likely to be trend-based, you'll need to commit to refreshing and updating them every season, so don't make this the bulk of your wardrobe, and certainly don't blow your budget on these pieces.

Look for a handful of accent clothing and accessories to add interest and pizzazz, based on the seasonal trends you're seeing in stores.

When selecting this 20 percent, try to buy within just two to three accent colors (pick colors that are in stores and on-trend for the season you're in). If you don't, you may end up with a random red bag, blue shoes, yellow belt, and green scarf, and you won't be able to pull these random colors together into a beautiful, cohesive outfit.

The 80/20 rule also explains why the majority of the pieces I've identified in the capsule wardrobe are largely in basic neutral colors, with only a few in accent colors or prints, because I'm applying the 80/20 rule to the thirty items in my capsule wardrobe.

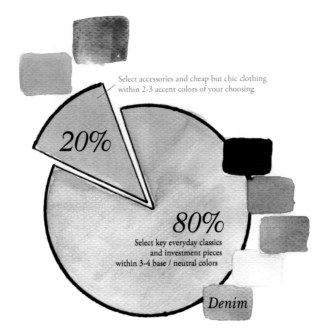

FIGURE 1: The 80/20 rule

DOES YOUR WARDROBE REFLECT YOUR LIFESTYLE?

The next little bit of planning you'll need to do for a successful wardrobe is a "wardrobe" versus "reality" analysis.

Think back for a moment to our two types of shoppers. We have Sparkling Sally, who buys lots and lots of pretty going-out clothing because she is attracted to beautiful, shiny things and hates buying "boring" stuff.

And then there's Boring Betty. She finds buying the basics easy because it's routine; shopping for anything else (like a dazzling dress) is too overwhelming to consider.

This usually results in a mismatch between what we own in our closets versus our actual needs in real life. Hence, we have to look at our wardrobe versus our reality.

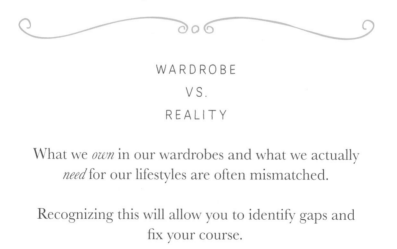

WARDROBE

VS.

REALITY

What we *own* in our wardrobes and what we actually *need* for our lifestyles are often mismatched.

Recognizing this will allow you to identify gaps and fix your course.

Here is an exercise that is super simple and worth taking the time to do. This is a useful tool will help you identify the extent of the mismatch between what you own (wardrobe) and what you actually need (reality).

Grab a blank sheet of paper and a pen, or a couple of different colored pencils or crayons—anything you have on hand.

First, think about a typical week in your life and work out how much of your time is spent wearing certain types of clothing. Start to map this out on your sheet of paper.

For example, do you spend 40 percent of your week at work? Maybe you spend another 10 percent of your week enjoying the occasional dry white wine over lunches and dinners with friends. And perhaps you spend 25 percent of your time in the playground running after the kids.

Finally, consider how much time you would spend running around doing chores or at the gym (although, let's be real, the only running you'd be doing is for a *big* sale at Christian Louboutin—not many of us look good in tight Lycra anyway!), and map all of this out on your sheet until all parts of your time are accounted for as a percentage (100 percent). This is the reality of what you do in a typical week.

Now, think about your actual wardrobe. How much of your wardrobe is apportioned to these different activities?

Does your wardrobe contain 40 percent of work wear and 25 percent of playground/weekend wear that you need to support your actual lifestyle? Or is there a mismatch in what you need vs. what you actually own in your closet?

In my experience, most of you will end up with something that looks like Figure 2: a misalignment between your reality (lifestyle) needs and what you have in your wardrobe.

So, it should come as no surprise that if what we have in our wardrobe doesn't match what we actually need in reality, the result is us standing in front of the closet every day, gasping, "I have *nothing* to wear!"

Once you recognize where you're wasting your precious moolah (for example, on more work clothes when you really don't need any more), you can correct your course and divert your shopping energy to what you actually need. You'll automatically know what to look for (and what to avoid!) the next time you're wandering through the mall.

FIGURE 2: Map out what you own in your wardrobe versus what you need in reality

Take a moment to do these planning exercises and you'll get one step closer to a well-balanced wardrobe, where you can mix and match foundational basics with fun, fashionable pieces to create a variety of looks for any occasion.

THE

Capsule
Wardrobe

FORMULA

Are you ready to start building a killer capsule wardrobe that will work for most of the events on your calendar?

When selecting the pieces for your wardrobe, the number one rule to remember is to select each item with purpose instead of randomly buying anything and everything that catches your eye.

THE CORE PRINCIPLES

Whether you subscribe to the thirty pieces I recommend in the following pages or you're creating your own capsule (or adjusting the list to accommodate your individual lifestyle or climate), there are a few principles to take to heart.

1. UNDERSTAND YOUR OWN BODY SHAPE

You understand your body best, so trust your instincts when selecting the pieces for your own capsule wardrobe. If there's a piece I suggest that you know won't look great on you, swap it for a slightly different shape (I do also include some alternate shapes for different bodies as we go along).

2. LEARN HOW TO WORK WITH COLOR

The main principle of a good capsule wardrobe is to work with having pieces for a light (warmer season) wardrobe and reflecting that with the dark (cooler season) wardrobe to match.

In essence, you want your winter and summer wardrobe to be a mirror of each other—similar pieces but in different colors.

Choose items in a lighter fabric and lighter color for the warmer weather, and heavier colors in weightier fabrics for the cooler months.

If we don't think about color, we end up with clothing that looks inappropriate for the weather—dark jackets and black dresses in the heat of summer or linen skirts in winter.

3. ADAPT FOR YOUR LIFESTYLE

The final items you choose for your capsule wardrobe may differ slightly from the ones I've suggested, depending on the nature of your lifestyle and where you live.

For example, if you're a full-time mom, then focus your wardrobe more on smart-casual and casual wear. You might want to replace the black skirt I suggest with a more casual skirt or shorts, or grab a second, lighter-colored ballet flat instead of black heels.

The capsule wardrobe also works heavily on the principle of layering, so you can get lots of wear out of all your items throughout the year. Of course, you'll need to add some additional pieces if you live in a particularly cold climate (I do have a chapter on colder climate dressing to help you decide what else you might need beginning on page 97).

LIGHT AND DARK

Mirror your pieces for the different seasons, i.e., similar style and cuts in lighter colors and fabrics for summer, and darker colors and warmer fabrics for winter!

START BUILDING YOUR CAPSULE WARDROBE!

To create the perfect capsule wardrobe, I've identified thirty basic pieces that can be mixed and matched to form over one thousand outfits!

I'll spend some time in the next chapter covering each of these pieces so you can learn why each one made the list. You'll also find the full list of all one thousand outfits at the back of this book on page 122, as a quick reference guide for when you next get dressed.

Take some time to see if you already own some of these pieces, and make a list of the ones you need to search for on your next shopping adventure.

As you do this, remember: the capsule wardrobe is more than what the actual pieces or outfits are. It's a way of living and styling yourself so you start to view your wardrobe differently—and more simplistically.

You will start becoming aware of how an easy addition or change (for example, swapping shoes or adding a necklace) can create a whole new look. Look at adding extra pieces (maybe an additional pair of pants) to help you create even more outfits than the thousand I have listed in this book.

THE CAPSULE WARDROBE FORMULA

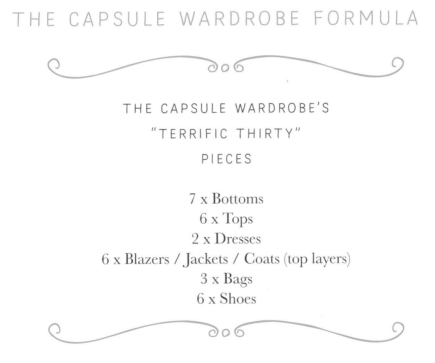

THE CAPSULE WARDROBE'S
"TERRIFIC THIRTY"
PIECES

7 x Bottoms
6 x Tops
2 x Dresses
6 x Blazers / Jackets / Coats (top layers)
3 x Bags
6 x Shoes

My "terrific thirty" items all mix and match into the ultimate capsule wardrobe to provide over one thousand outfit combinations.

The formula is simple.

All tops must match all bottoms. Plus, each jacket or coat also matches all our tops and bottoms.

Add to that a good selection of shoes and bags and you have yourself a healthy combination of outfits.

Now, I promise that this is the only time I'll get all mathematical on you. With some simple multiplication, you'll see that for every extra top you add you'll easily get another thirty-five combinations—just from one additional blouse!

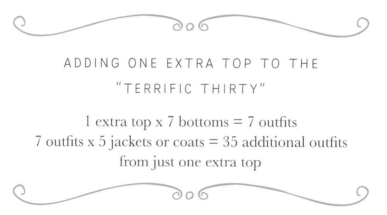

ADDING ONE EXTRA TOP TO THE
"TERRIFIC THIRTY"

1 extra top x 7 bottoms = 7 outfits
7 outfits x 5 jackets or coats = 35 additional outfits
from just one extra top

Choosing a dress instead of a top or bottom will reduce the total number of outfits you can create, but it's important to still have some dresses for variety. Just make sure they work with all your jackets, too.

Now, let's take a look at each of the thirty pieces in our capsule wardrobe in more detail.

THE CAPSULE WARDROBE'S
"Terrific Thirty"

It's time to dive in and find out exactly what terrific thirty pieces make up the capsule wardrobe!

BOTTOMS

First, we're going to start with bottoms, which are the base of your entire wardrobe and the foundation for each outfit.

I've selected two pairs of pants (or trousers, depending on where you're from) in black and a lighter color, such as stone. Both should ideally have belt loops unless you carry the majority of your weight in the midsection and rarely wear belts.

TROUSERS, PANTS, SKIRTS, AND SHORTS

1 x tailored pants in black

1 x tailored pants in stone

1 x casual pants in taupe/mushroom (a skinny cut is
the most versatile)

1 x pair jeans in dark indigo wash

1 x tailored, but not "suit" style, black skirt

1 x casual skirt (denim, stretch cotton, or linen)

1 x pair stone shorts

Select cuts that best suit your body shape and that
can also be worn casually (i.e., not too formal)

TAILORED PANTS—BLACK

Your black pants should be a classic cut and smartly tailored in a dressier fabric. This will allow us to take it from work to evening.

Alternatives: Choose between a tapered (skinny) leg or a wider cut depending on your silhouette.

FIGURE 3: Tailored straight-leg pants   **FIGURE 4:** Skinny or tapered-leg pants

TAILORED PANTS—STONE

Your lighter color pants could be stone, cream, off-white, pale gray, or a very light brown—whatever appeals to you most.

Personally, I think stone is the most versatile, which is why it's my top pick.

Choose a pair in a slightly more casual fabric than your tailored black pants. This will prove useful when it comes to utilizing these pants in your weekend wear.

FIGURE 5: Lighter colored tailored pants

It could be a cotton fabric or have a slight print pattern such as a herringbone or a weave. Fabric is important here because we don't want you to look like you're wearing one half of a bad, shiny polyester Miami Vice cream suit!

Alternatives: Once again, you could choose a skinnier or wider leg depending on your preference.

CASUAL PANTS—TAUPE

Whether you choose a pair in gray, brown, or taupe/khaki, try to choose a skinny cut style if possible. (Before you bail on this book for using the words "skinny cut," just hang in there. In the next section on jeans, I explain why a skinny cut can be good!)

This is a pair of pants that you can wear really, really casually. It is a great option for in-between seasonal weather.

Because they're perfect for casual activities and running around, a skinny leg is an especially great cut as it works very well with flat shoes. They make your legs look leaner and your overall silhouette sharper. They are much more flattering when worn with flats compared to a boot or wide-leg cut.

Choose a pair in a shade like taupe (also sometimes called *mushroom*). Not as dull as gray, not as drab as brown, and not as light as stone,

FIGURE 6: Taupe casual pants

taupe (or mushroom) is a great color as it matches really well with black but is light enough to match with a stone blazer.

(You don't want to wear stone slacks and stone blazers together—it's a bit like double denim, which is a big no-no unless you really know what you're doing. I still don't care what the latest fashion magazine says!)

JEANS

Love 'em or hate 'em, we can't seem to get by without 'em. The most useful pair of jeans to own is one in a super dark indigo wash. Dark jeans are easier to dress up as opposed to a light wash jean, which can sometimes be too casual.

FIGURE 7: Dark skinny jeans

Look for a mid-rise to tuck our "I shouldn't have had that chocolate cake but I did" muffin tops in. Also look for a skinny cut leg.

Now, please don't panic—there *are* ways for almost anyone to wear a skinny jean, even if you are scared of the sight of your denim-clad bottom!

Why a skinny leg? (I can still hear wails of horror and the sound of some readers slapping this book down in disgust. Stay with me, though!)

Firstly, skinny legs mean you'll be able to tuck your jeans into knee-high boots during the depths of winter, which gives you infinitely more combinations to wear.

Secondly, a more tapered leg will match better with blousier, volumi-nous tops. It's all about proportion—if we go a little looser at the top (which we tend to do because most of us are trying to hide a tummy, hips, or bum), then we need a sexier shape in our bottom half. And that is what a nice, tapered skinny leg will do for us. If not, we'll end up looking like a sack with our wide top and wide jeans!

Thirdly, you never have to wear anything tucked into your skinny jeans, and you can always have a blazer, cardigan, or little jacket to go over your jeans, giving you some coverage over the tummy and waist area.

Alternatives: If your shape genuinely isn't flattered by a skinny-legged jean, then please feel free to choose a wider or straight leg, but do try to ensure the tops you wear with it aren't too baggy.

STYLE TIP

For most, the best place to end your tops and jackets
is approximately midway down your bum.

Just long enough to cover any bumps around the
waist or midsection, but short enough to show off
the shape of your bottom.

BLACK SKIRT

A black skirt that can be dressed up for work and then worn to a more
formal evening out is ideal.

FIGURE 8: Black pencil skirt

Look for some kind of detail to the skirt to make it less office-like. You'll find it to be more versatile when transitioning from work to a night out.

For example, look for a shuttered skirt, a skirt with a little ruffle at the hem, or one with an interesting waist detail—anything that doesn't shout, "I'm a boring work skirt," but that can still be worn in a work environment.

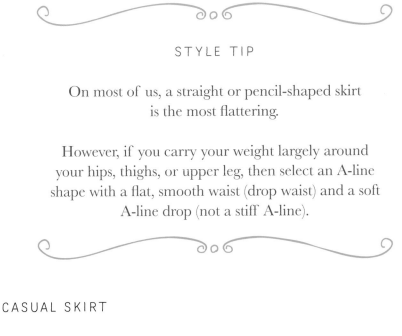

STYLE TIP

On most of us, a straight or pencil-shaped skirt is the most flattering.

However, if you carry your weight largely around your hips, thighs, or upper leg, then select an A-line shape with a flat, smooth waist (drop waist) and a soft A-line drop (not a stiff A-line).

CASUAL SKIRT

This is the kind of skirt you can wear during the summer for a BBQ or picnic. I recommend a denim skirt in a pencil or straight cut (what I fondly call the "grown up" denim skirt).

The trick is to keep it simple, so steer away from embellishments, buttons, stitching, and other details. Again, look for a skirt in a very dark indigo wash.

A simple denim skirt can be worn to the park on the weekend with your trusty sandals, *or* you can wear it with opaque tights and knee-high boots for winter.

FIGURE 9: Dark wash straight or pencil denim skirt

Alternative: If you best suit an A-line skirt, don't select one in denim. Denim is too stiff a fabric to make for a soft drop in an A-line, so you'll end up with a large, unflattering, boxy skirt. Much better to look at a different fabric instead that will allow for a softer drop in this shape. Instead, pick light, breezy fabrics that will fall naturally, like the ones pictured in Figures 10 or 11.

FIGURE 10: Casual A-line, alternative 1   **FIGURE 11:** Casual A-line, alternative 2

SHORTS

The perfect antidote for summer weather. In the heat, shorts are the answer!

Pick a stone or cream pair (or even a soft, dusty pink) over black because, while there are ways to dress up stone shorts for summer evenings, it's harder to make black, heat-absorbing shorts work on a bright, sunny day when it's ninety degrees outside.

If you can find them, cuffed shorts work really well. They have a slightly more tailored look, which means you can wear them dressed up with wedges and a light blazer.

If you don't like your knees or legs, select a pair of long shorts (just past the knee), but do not be tempted to replace shorts with three-quarter pants or trousers. This is the most unflattering length of pants anyone can own (and I've seen a lot of them lurking in many wardrobes, waiting to come out and shame their owners!).

If you really need to, go for a proper seven-eighth length pair of pants rather than the in-between length of three-quarters. As I always say, sometimes you have to pick and commit to a team. Decide if they're either shorts or proper pants, but don't leave it hanging somewhere in the middle.

We now have pants for work and weekend and for summer and winter. We have skirts for work and play that can be worn in warm or cool months. We also have a pair of shorts for those truly hot casual days. And that's just with our first seven items. So far, we're off to a good start. Now, let's look at what you'll need in terms of tops, jackets, and coats.

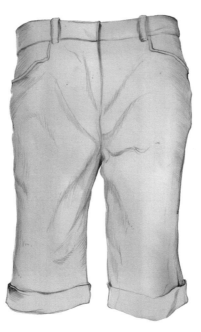

FIGURE 12: Tailored light-colored shorts

TOPS, BLOUSES, AND BLAZERS

TOPS, BLOUSES, AND BLAZERS

2 x long-sleeved tops (black or white + accent color)

2 x basic tank tops for summer

2 x accent-colored blouses in a dressy, smart
fabric to suit all occasions

2 x blazers (black and stone) that fit and flatter your
shape to take you from work to play

1 x black cardigan that isn't too baggy or frumpy

LONG-SLEEVED CLASSIC TOPS—
BLACK AND ACCENT COLORS

You'll need two of these classic tops. Both should have a neckline that flatters you, be it a wide scoop or a V-neck. Ideally, stay away from a very high round neck as this makes the top harder to layer when the high neck risks peeking out from under your other clothes.

A black top is essential. I'm sure you can see how easily you could match that with lots of outfits, although you could swap it out for a white if you prefer. In black, this top can be layered underneath dresses, taking them from summer to winter.

FIGURE 13: Classic top in black

FIGURE 14: Classic sleeved top in an accent color

FIGURE 15: An alternative to an accent color is a Breton-style tee

Ensure that you're not selecting anything too bulky fabric-wise that could make it hard to layer. I have selected a long-sleeved top; however, if you live in a warmer climate or don't like that style, choose a short-sleeved top instead.

The second piece is a top in a similar style, but in an accent color. An accent color is a color that keeps your wardrobe interesting outside of the basic black, white, and gray. It could be a bright blue, a stunning coral, or even a sexy red—whatever you have decided are your best colors. (Remember our 80/20 rule? This colorful top falls in the fun, funky 20 percent of your wardrobe.)

Alternative: If a block color isn't your thing, choose a Breton-style (striped) tee as an option.

BASIC TANK TOPS—BLACK AND WHITE

You'll need two tanks, in black and white or off-white (see figures 16 and 17 on the next page). These are tops you can throw on with your shorts or denim skirt to skip down to the shop for your Sunday paper, or wear underneath a blazer on a Monday at work.

Make sure that the straps are wide enough to cover a bra strap for maximum versatility.

Alternative: If you are conscious of how your arms look, or if you live in a cooler climate, go for a top in a thicker weight or one that comes with a sleeve.

ACCENT-COLORED BLOUSES

At a minimum, I'd pick two blouses in a fabric such as satin or silk (or one that looks like a satin or silk to keep costs down). These will smarten up your wardrobe compared to the plain cotton or jersey tanks and tops from the previous pages.

For most people, the challenge with smart casual is often in the fabric of their tops.

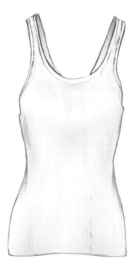

FIGURE 16: Black tank

FIGURE 17: White tank

When I encounter a client who wants to smarten up their weekend wardrobe, they usually don't mean that they'd like to rock up in a little, low-cut black dress for lunch with the in-laws or a PTA meeting, but they also don't feel that a plain cotton tee and jeans do them enough justice.

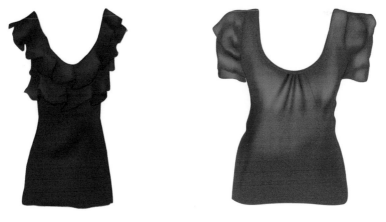

FIGURE 18: Accent
blouse, option 1

FIGURE 19: Accent
blouse, option 2

This is where a nice blouse in a dressier fabric, such as satin or silk, will do the trick. The nicer fabric will dress up any pair of shorts, jeans, or casual skirt. Plus, it'll go the distance when it comes to work wear as well.

Select blouses that can be worn untucked over your taupe casual pants or jeans, or tucked into a skirt or black pants for work. The final test is to ensure the blouses sit well when you throw on a blazer or lightweight jacket.

Choose tops in two bright accent colors (try prints if you feel confident enough). These will fall into the trendy or seasonal portion of your wardrobe (the 20 percent in our trusty 80/20 rule).

To extend your wardrobe even further and give yourself more outfits, simply add a couple more tops to your capsule.

STYLE TIP

Choose a blouse with a little cap sleeve or short sleeve if you wish to cover your arms, and adapt the neckline to best suit your figure.

Adding a few extra tops is the fastest way to create more outfits in your capsule wardrobe.

BLAZERS—BLACK AND STONE

As you've probably guessed by now, I'm not a fan of the traditional matching suit. It's too restrictive and very hard to mix and match with more casual pieces. However, we all need a jacket look from time to time. To achieve this, simply grab a couple of blazers in stone or off-white and black. (If black isn't your color, try deep charcoal or navy.)

The trick is to select blazers that can take you from the boardroom with a black tailored skirt to a few red wines on a Friday evening when worn with jeans.

For that reason, don't choose a blazer that looks too tailored or business-like. Things such as a high neckline (the giveaway is usually more than three buttons) can make a jacket look more office than dressy.

Ideally, look for blazers that taper in at your waist and back, and are fitted around the arms to show off your shape. Judge your blazer on what it looks like open, which you'll probably do more often with jeans or pants. If it's fitted enough, it should sit well open over a blouse for work.

Details like ruched sleeves, or a slight peplum or ruffle will help make the blazer look smart but not office-y.

FIGURE 20: Black blazer   **FIGURE 21:** Stone blazer

THE CARDIGAN—BLACK

I'm not going to lie, this one's tricky. Select the right cardigan and it'll be your best friend and an integral part of your trans-seasonal wardrobe. Select the wrong one, however, and you could look like your grandmother (we love her, but you don't need to dress like her).

The trick is to start with a three-quarter or shorter sleeve. This is infinitely more modern and contemporary than a full length sleeve as it will show off your slender wrists. Then, look for a wide-open scoop neck or a V-neck. Round high neck cardigans are the domain of wee, little elderly women. You'll have plenty of time for that in the future!

The final tip is to look for a cardigan that is quite fitted, so we can see your shape (avoid one that is too long).

Now, we have nine delightful tops that will (amazingly) take you from top-tier work meetings to lunch with your girlfriends, last-minute desperation shopping at the local gas station for chocolate, school runs, playground dates, and cocktails with hubby!

We're starting to really rock 'n' roll!

Pants, jeans, skirts, and shorts? Check!

Tanks, tees, blouses, and blazers? Check and check!

It's time for dresses.

FIGURE 22: Fitted black cardigan

DRESSES

DRESSES

1 x LBD for day to night

1 x casual printed dress for daytime pleasures

THE LITTLE BLACK DRESS—GO FROM WORK TO GLAM

Little black dresses (**LBD**) never go out of style and are crucial to your desk-to-dazzling, day-to-night ensembles.

The first piece you'll need is a dress that is office or work appropriate. Things to look for include: a little sleeve (which means you can wear it on its own during summer or layer it over a long-sleeved black tee for winter) and a hem length that ends just near the knee (below if you really don't like your knees) so it's not too dowdy, but still work appropriate.

Change into the right footwear and accessories and, voila, you're off to the theater or a formal evening out, straight from the office.

FIGURE 23A: Desk-to-dazzling little black dress, option 1

FIGURE 23B: Desk-to-dazzling little black dress, option 2

THE CASUAL DAY DRESS

What should you wear when the in-laws come over for lunch? Or when you are popping out for a spot of Saturday shopping with the gals?

A casual daytime dress, of course!

If you're feeling bold enough to experiment, look for a printed dress with a pattern (I know some people are scared of patterns, but there's nothing to fear!).

When selected correctly, patterns can be very forgiving and camouflaging of lumps and bumps. Patterns that are small, repetitive, and low in color contrast are best. Big, bright, clown-like patterns are the ones to avoid.

Patterns usually mean that many different colors are used in the print, making it easier to match with various colors and accessories.

FIGURE 24: Casual day dress, option 1 in a print

FIGURE 25: Casual day dress, option 2 in a block color

I've included two very different style of dresses here—depending on your age, shape, and personal taste—that both hit the mark in terms of versatility to make it work as part of a true capsule wardrobe.

Alternative: If patterns really scare you, select a block color, but don't pick anything too bold as it'll be too hard to

match with other colors. Additionally, if you carry your weight through your hips and thighs, you may wish to select a dress with a more fluid, floaty skirt.

JACKETS AND COATS

JACKETS & COATS

1 x classic trench
1 x winter parka
1 x lightweight jacket for in-between seasons

Substitute these for other tops or bottoms if you live in a warm area, or add more pieces if you need them for winter!

You'll need three jackets: a classic trench ideal for most occasions, a proper winter parka-style jacket for the coldest of days, and a casual, lightweight jacket for all those in-between seasons.

Your casual jacket should not be too long (the shorter it is, the easier it'll be to wear with shorts or skirts). The color should be versatile, such as olive or a dusty gold.

Alternative: If you live in a very cold climate, add as many coats as you need to accommodate. Conversely, if you live in a very warm area, you can drop the jackets and coats and substitute them for additional tops or bottoms!

FIGURE 26: Classic trench coat

FIGURE 27: Casual, lightweight jacket

FIGURE 28: Warm, winter-weight parka

We've conquered the basics and essentials of the apparel we need. Now, let's progress to the wonderful world of every woman's dreams . . . *shoes*!

SHOES

SHOES

1 x pair patent black pumps

1 x pair strappy black sandals

1 x boots in black (knee-high or ankle-length depending on climate)

1 x dressy flat sandals

1 x black ballet flats

1 x tan pair of wedges

Unbelievably, this capsule wardrobe streamlines our shoe-drobe to just six essential pairs.

Before you start to hurl your Manolos at me, know that you don't have to feel limited to just six pairs. In the spirit of minimalism, you could get by with no more than that *if* you really need to, but I know most of us need shoes to live, breathe, and survive. If that's you, feel free to add more shoes to your collection.

For now, we're going to look at the pairs you need as an absolute minimum for your capsule wardrobe.

BLACK PUMPS

First up, you need a nice black pump, as high (or low) as you're comfortable with. If you can't wear heels, select a wedge heel instead.

Ideally, I'd recommend a patent leather—the shinier the shoe, the better it is for more formal occasions. I also prefer a slightly rounded toe as this can then be worn on its own during summer or with tights or stockings during winter. A pointed toe can look a tad odd with winter tights.

FIGURE 29: Black heels in patent leather, as low or high as is comfortable

STRAPPY BLACK HEELS

The next are what I call *sexy heels*. This needs to be an open, strappy, sandal-style heel. Heels that will be your go-to pair for nights out. They should look great peeking out from under pants and jeans, and they are crucial for those little black dresses!

If you don't have much occasion to wear these heels, swap for another pair of flats, wedges, or even boots, depending on your lifestyle and climate.

FIGURE 30A: Strappy heels for going out, option 1

FIGURE 30B: Strappy heels for going out, option 2

BLACK BOOTS

Unless you live in a warm, tropical climate, a boot is essential. If you can only include one pair in your capsule wardrobe, then choose between a knee-high version or an ankle-length depending on how cold it gets where you live.

Either way, don't pick anything with lots of embellishment (this means no buckles, chains, buttons, or any "bits")—these will date the boot and make it hard to match with anything else.

Select a flat boot or a heel if you can manage it. Once again, I love patent leather, so as the head of the patent leather fan club, I say try to find a patent pair to make it easy taking the boot from day to night. Check that you can tuck your (skinny) jeans into the boots for maximum versatility.

If you live in a warm climate, replace the boots with another pair of sandals or wedges.

FIGURE 31: Black knee-high boots in patent leather

FIGURE 32: Ankle-length boots as an alternative if you don't need a knee-high pair

BALLET FLATS

For those days off, we all need a pair of reliable flats. And as much as trends like brogues or loafers come and go, a ballet flat is a classic staple that seems to defy trends.

Whether you choose a pair in plain leather or snakeskin, ballet flats are flattering, comfortable, and equally versatile with skirts, dresses, pants, or jeans. While a rounded toe is always popular, a pointed flat can be a great option as well.

FIGURE 33: Flats to run around in

DRESSY FLAT SANDALS

For those lazy, hazy summer days, we need a pair of good old flat sandals. But forget those shabby rubber flip flops we try to pass off on vacation from beach to bars, as they don't really spell *style*.

Instead, choose a dressy pair of flat sandals in a metallic gold or silver, and they will take you from sand to Saturday night in a flash.

FIGURE 34: Dressy gold flat sandals   **FIGURE 35:** Dressy silver flat sandals

NUDE WEDGES

Finally, don't forget the essential nude or tan wedge.

This will be your summer go-to for casual lunches, drinks under the stars, and the office. Once again (yes, yes, broken record): *patent leather rocks*, so if you find a shiny pair in nude patent—grab it!

FIGURE 36: Tan or nude wedges

BAGS

From shoes we move on to the other *great* obsession of women—bags, bags, bags (a close second was chocolate, of course).

Like shoes, you don't need many, but you do need to make an effort to change bags.

I know what it's like to change handbags and find you've left your house keys or subway pass in the other, but my mom taught me an easy solution. She's introduced me to little make-up zip cases for everything—one for makeup, one for keys and travel tickets, another for tissues and breath mints, and so on. Having four or five little pouches that you can easily transfer from bag to bag means that trying to break into your own home because you forgot the keys will be a thing of the past!

Bags essentially need to complement shoes. So, all you need is a black tote (to complement our black shoes) plus a tan or beige tote to complement our nude/summer shoes, and finally a little black clutch for nights out!

FIGURE 37: Tan tote bag

FIGURE 38: A classic black tote for everyday wear

FIGURE 39: A little black clutch for nights out

FIGURE 40: Alternative tote bag in tan with silver accents

COLOR CONSIDERATIONS

If you don't like black or can't wear black, then choose colors like charcoal or lighter gray marl instead of black.

If you're not a fan of white, look for a cream, light beige, or mushroom. And if you don't like stone, select a soft, dusty pink instead.

PUTTING IT ALL TOGETHER

Wow, we are done!

That's all of the thirty pieces you need to create your new capsule wardrobe, aka the "terrific thirty"!

With these power pieces, you can have a fabulous wardrobe with minimal clutter, and you won't have to re-mortgage your house or sell your first-born child. You'll get maximum wear from mixing and matching these thirty individual items in a thousand ways!

Remember—add and adjust to the list as you need to account for your own taste, style, body shape, lifestyle, and, of course, weather.

In the next chapter, I'll show you how your thirty pieces can mix and match together.

YOUR SPECIAL STYLE BONUS

I know that dragging this book around when you're out shopping can be a little impractical.

So I've created a handy pocket guide with a list (and illustrations) of each of the capsule wardrobe pieces so you can refer to it easily when shopping!

You can download your free copy at:

www.wendymak.com/capsulewardrobepocketguide

THE ART OF
Mixing and Matching

Now that we've taken a detailed look at each item in your capsule wardrobe, it's time to learn how to use them.

Ultimately, this is all about optimizing your wardrobe—reusing and reworking the same items in clever, smart, and sometimes unexpected ways.

This chapter will show you how to approach mixing and matching. Additionally, I'll introduce you to the value and importance of accessories when it comes to transforming your outfits.

Let's start simple. In Figure 41, our tailored stone pants are matched with the white cotton tank. Throw the black blazer over it and finish the look with black pumps/heels and a black tote. Perfect for the office!

In Figure 42, I swap out the black shoes and bag from Figure 41 for tan wedges and a tan tote, making this appropriate for a hot summer's day with lighter toned accessories (and, if you need it, use the blazer for the frosty temperatures of the office air conditioning!).

FIGURE 41   **FIGURE 42**

Keeping most things the same, in Figure 43 I simply change the blazer to a more casual jacket. The outfit is now weekend-ready for shopping, a brunch, or even casual Friday at the office.

As you can see from these examples, by making easy swaps with your jackets or blazers, shoes, and bags, the basic white tank and stone pants outfit quickly transforms into three completely different outfits.

Let's take this concept a step further.

FIGURE 43   **FIGURE 44**

Figure 44 retains the same stone pants, taken up a notch when paired with an accent colored blouse. With a black blazer, shoes, and black tote, this is ready for work.

Now, watch what happens when I change a core item—pants to shorts—in this outfit. Retaining the same top, the look transforms into smart summer chic when worn with a pair of stone shorts instead of pants. All you need to finish are tan wedges and a tan tote (Figure 45).

By now you should start to see how interchangeable our items are and how a quick change of shoes and bags can transform an outfit.

FIGURE 45 **FIGURE 46**

The common factor with all our outfits is color. If you have at least two light or dark elements in your combination, then you have an outfit (as opposed to a haphazard mash of random items).

Let's explore how the concept of having at least one light item with another light item (or one dark with dark) actually works, utilizing our day dress as an example.

On its own, the most basic look is to style our dress with shoes and a bag—in this case, our tan shoes and tan bag, two light colored items, in Figure 46.

The dress takes on a completely different look when we match our stone blazer (one light item) with the tan shoes and tan bag (our second and third light colored items) in Figure 47.

The addition of the stone blazer easily makes this a work-appropriate outfit for spring or summer, and even warmer winter days if you live in a more temperate climate.

When we change the blazer and bag to black versions, and add black knee-high boots, the outfit is instantly transformed into something more dramatic and formal (Figure 48).

FIGURE 47   **FIGURE 48**

There's the minimum of two dark items to pull the look together, but the overall darker colors add a whole different dimension. This is definitely a winter-ready outfit (I've added a belt over the blazer, too, to keep it looking interesting—more on accessories later in this book).

STYLE TIP

The more colors in the print of your dress, the more versatile it is. It'll be easier to match with more colors and accessories.

Keep the print pattern small to flatter and camouflage lumps and bumps.

THE WARDROBE FOR
Success

Crafting the perfect look for the office doesn't have to be an exercise in futility.

Let's look at some potential combinations that are perfect choices for office attire.

THE LBD FOR WORK

We love our basic little black dress (**LBD**) for work—pull it on, slap on some shoes, grab a bag, throw on a blazer, and you're good to go, easy as one-two-three (Figure 49).

Our black dress can also be styled up for the cold depths of winter. In Figure 50, I've layered the dress over a black long-sleeved top. The dress is instantly transformed from a short-sleeved dress into a winter outfit. Knee-high black boots, a black bag, and a coat complete this look for those cold days.

As a final touch, I've thrown on a little neck scarf just to give you an idea of how to incorporate an accessory into the outfit.

FIGURE 49   **FIGURE 50**

CHANGING THE LOOK WITH ACCESSORIES

Work wear can often be uninspiring, and our ability to be creative and express our individuality usually comes from our use of accessories. Let's explore how we can use accessories for work.

In both Figures 51 and 52, I use the basic stone tailored pants, worn with a white tank, black blazer, black pumps, and tote bag.

Here's how much accessories can change the look. In Figure 51, I've used a scarf to add some color and warmth to the outfit, whereas Figure 52 is a more classic look with a short, colored necklace and a skinny blue belt for a shot of color.

As you can see, subtle changes can make a big impact on any outfit.

FIGURE 51   **FIGURE 52**

Meanwhile, our black pants take on a smart but chic summer look when worn with the white tank, stone blazer, tan bag, and wedges (Figure 53).

When we swap the top to an accent colored blue long-sleeved top, and throw in a matching little blue belt and the trusty black blazer from our capsule wardrobe, we now have a different look that takes on a "darker" feel—perfect for cooler months (Figure 54).

Our black pants now gives us two very different outfits!

FIGURE 53   FIGURE 54

THREE LOOKS, ONE BLACK SKIRT

Let's take a closer look at our black skirt. The skirt in our capsule wardrobe is a layered, shutter-style skirt. With this detailing, it doesn't look like a boring black pencil work skirt. This allows me to style it for occasions outside of work, with the right accompanying pieces.

Figure 55 features another simple but lovely work outfit using the black skirt, an accent colored blouse, tan shoes, and a tan bag.

FIGURE 55: Three ways with a black skirt, option 1

Figure 56 pictures the reverse. We've now paired the same ensemble of skirt and blouse, but this time with black shoes and a black bag. Also, I now have the stone blazer as an accent piece.

Meanwhile, Figure 57 shows a completely different look for the black skirt. This time, the skirt is transformed into a more formal look, appropriate for an important meeting, with the addition of the black blazer, a long-sleeved colored top, and a few accessories such as a belt and a necklace.

FIGURE 56: Three ways with a black skirt, option 2

FIGURE 57: Three ways with a black skirt, option 3

Now that you've mastered your work wardrobe, we'll delve into the world of fashion for a night out on the town in the next chapter.

OUT ON THE

Town

Dressing for a night out can be a lot of fun. Our capsule wardrobe will give you a range of choices to pick from so you can go from desk to dazzling in minutes!

Going out can span many different types of occasions. The beauty of your new wardrobe is that whether it's cocktail or casual chic, you'll have the pieces you need to create a perfect combination.

THE LBD—RESTYLED FOR NIGHTS OUT

Remember our little black dress for work? Well, it's back, but not as you've seen it before.

With a quick change to our strappy black heels and little black clutch, this outfit (Figure 58) is an instant after-five wonder. All you need to finish this look are a pair of earrings and a little waist belt. Choose any belt that has more sparkle and evening chic to it (bring out the Sparkling Sally in yourself!).

And if you thought a simple black tank and tailored slacks were boring, take a closer look. All the outfit needs are a pair of sexy heels, a sexier little bag, and a couple of fun accessories, such as a bangle and earrings for a bit of evening va-va-voom (Figure 59).

FIGURE 58: A small clutch and a little bling transforms your work LBD to nighttime chic

FIGURE 59: A simple tank and pants becomes elegant chic

SMART CASUAL CHIC

For more casual (but no less important!) occasions, Figure 60 shows how a trusty white tank and black blazer can turn in to a super summer look by wearing it with stone tailored shorts, black heels and clutch.

FIGURE 60: Smart casual summer chic

Jeans have always been a smart casual staple—and here they reign again in three very different examples.

First, jeans with one of the accent colored blouses, strappy heels, a black clutch, and the black blazer (who said blazers were just for the office?) makes a wonderful evening outfit (Figure 61).

A quick change back to one of our colored tops, parka, and a swift tucking of the jeans into knee-high boots (see, those skinny jeans worked out in the end), topped with a warm hat completes our second outfit in Figure 62.

Finally, our original combination in Figure 61 takes on a new look and more casual feel when paired with a larger handbag and wedges. Or, keep the look smart by finishing it with a stone blazer (Figure 63).

FIGURE 61: Three ways with jeans, option 1

89

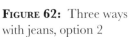

FIGURE 62: Three ways with jeans, option 2

FIGURE 63: Three ways with jeans, option 3

EVERY GIRL NEEDS A

Day Off

Tempting as it might be on your days off to slip on a pair of sweats and your favorite hoodie, it really would make Anna Wintour wince—and if she has made a facial expression, that is *big* news.

The better news is that your thirty capsule wardrobe pieces have you covered!

SUMMER STYLE FOR THOSE DAYS OFF

Figure 64 pictures the now familiar combination of stone tailored pants and white tank, but this time teamed with a casual lightweight jacket, ballet flats (a stylish alternative to tennis shoes), and a black tote—perfect for casual Sunday lunch.

In Figure 65, the stone shorts make for a super casual look with an accent colored long-sleeved tee, flat dressy sandals, and a tan tote. A picnic or quick run to get gas and groceries never looked better!

FIGURE 64: Casual summer chic, option 1

FIGURE 65: Casual summer chic, option 2

Figure 66 shows how an outfit with the same shorts completely changes when worn with a basic white tank and a simple necklace for a splash of color.

And then, simply by changing to stone casual pants, we have yet another outfit (Figure 67).

FIGURE 66: Casual summer chic, option 3

FIGURE 67: Casual summer chic, option 4

By now, you should be getting inspired and seeing the multitude of combinations you can create for those casual days from just thirty well-selected items.

CASUAL CHIC FOR COOLER DAYS

As summer fades away, we start to move toward darker colors and accents. Remember that our winter and summer wardrobes should mirror each other—light and dark to suit the warm and cold seasons.

A casual day dress paired with black ballet flats, a black tote, and cardigan is the perfect answer to the last days of summer or fall blues.

An easy trick to create and show off as much of your shape as possible (so that your cardigan looks more glam than grandma) is to place a little belt around it to emphasize the waist (Figure 68).

Another warmer option that is casual, but still funky, uses the same flats and bag, but is matched with jeans, a blouse, and a parka (Figure 69).

FIGURE 68: Use a belt over jackets and cardigans to create shape

FIGURE 69: Jeans and a parka for cooler days

For other casually elegant options, try the denim skirt with a long-sleeved black top. Top it off with a casual jacket, knee-high boots, and a scarf (Figure 70).

As you can see, there are many ways to combine your thirty pieces into outfits that take you from summer, winter, days on, days off, and everything else in between!

FIGURE 70: The denim skirt works for both summer and winter

Winter Wonderland

Those of us who live in very cold climates will need to add a few extra pieces in order to complete the capsule wardrobe.

Before we dive in, remember that it's important to adjust your winter wardrobe selections based on your climate. Use this chapter as a guide to help you discover the key pieces for colder wear, but adjust the length, weight, insulation, and even number of items based on how cold it gets and the duration of your winter.

THERMALS AND LAYERS

The first addition you'll need to make are thermals. Granted, these won't get seen as part of your outfits necessarily, but they're still a critical part of creating a warm wardrobe to ward off the deep winter chill.

The good news is thermals don't have to be boring and dull. They now come in a wide range of styles, colors, and prints (Figure 71).

FIGURE 71: Look for fun thermals to lighten up winter days

SWEATERS AND COATS

The next key additions are a couple of sweaters. Because our capsule wardrobe has a couple of long-sleeved tops in basic colors, you can afford to look for sweaters in accent colors.

This will help add a pop of color to dark jeans, black parkas, etc.

Here, I've chosen two sweaters, a cable-knit turtleneck in a soft blush pink (useful for casual days off and weekends), and a more elegant sweater in light gray that can be dressed up for work and going out (Figures 72 and 73).

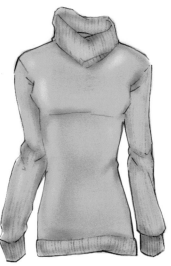

FIGURE 72: Pick a more casual sweater in an accent color

FIGURE 73: Wear an elegant sweater for nights out and work

FIGURE 74: A wool or cashmere coat for dressier days

Finally, consider adding a heavy winter-weight coat to your coat collection to complement the lighter jackets and casual parka in your current capsule wardrobe. In comparison to the parka, this coat will serve you well as a dressier option for outerwear. Look for something that is neutral in color, for example, a camel-colored wool coat in Figure 74.

BOOTS (AND MORE BOOTS!)

We already have a pair of knee-high black boots as part of our capsule wardrobe. If you live in a colder climate, add a couple more pairs of boots to your shoe collection.

You could choose another knee-high pair; however, in this case I've gone with a few ankle-length options for running around in—a black moto-style flat boot (seen earlier in the book as an alternative to knee-highs) and a tan pair (Figures 75 and 76).

FIGURE 75: A flat black ankle boot to round out your shoe-drobe

FIGURE 76: Tan or brown boots will also serve you well

WINTER OUTFIT IDEAS

With these few additions (plus a few more accessories, such as scarves and hats, which we'll cover in the next chapter), you can create a multitude of winter-friendly outfits.

For example, Figure 77 takes the black skirt from our capsule wardrobe and pairs it with thick tights, a white top, and the gray sweater. A necklace and black ankle boots complete the look. Just throw on appropriate outerwear and you're ready for dinner out or a smart casual workday.

FIGURE 77: Winter outfit ideas, option 1

FIGURE 78: Winter outfit ideas, option 2

Then, swap the skirt and tights for jeans and tan ankle boots, plus a scarf and coat, and our gray sweater takes on a more casual flair (Figure 78).

For an even more casual everyday outfit, the cable-knit sweater with stone pants and tan boots, topped with a winter hat, will have you out and about in no time (Figure 79).

FIGURE 79: Winter outfit ideas, option 3

Remember, the key is to assess your own individual lifestyle and climate to make the appropriate adjustments to your capsule winter wardrobe. If you need to, swap out some of the warmer climate pieces for more winter-style pieces.

ACCESSORIES:
The Finishing Touch

Accessories (shoes, bags, scarves, jewelry, hats, and belts) are a wonderful addition to your capsule wardrobe of staples.

They are the finishing touch with the ability to instantly transform an outfit from ordinary into something quite special.

It's a trick that I often use with much success—stretching my fashion budget a lot further by choosing very simple, basic items of clothing and getting multiple outfits and looks from big, bold statement accessories. This way, your clothes become almost like a plain canvas, and you "paint" your canvas with your accessories!

And that's the true beauty of accessories—they can be anything from a dollar item at a garage sale to those ridiculously expensive, yet gloriously Elizabeth Taylor-esque baubles. You can easily tailor your selection to suit your budget and tastes.

YOU CAN NEVER HAVE TOO MUCH BLING

While I've selected some essential shoes and bags that you'll need to make your capsule wardrobe work, feel free to add (modestly!) to your accessory collection as they help turn your capsule clothing into different looks.

When it comes to shoes, bags, and jewels, you won't get any judgment from me (or anyone else really, because we all deserve a bag here and there to light up our lives)! Owning multiple accessories is your right, just as it is your right to crave chocolate at any time of the day.

Having said that, don't become too much of a hoarder with accessories for they, too, can date (and break!) and clutter your capsule wardrobe. Always refine your collection of accessories, toss out the old, and look for new updates every season.

Accessories are the simplest, fastest, and often most affordable way to change and liven up your wardrobe! There's no need to shy away from regularly updating your accessories.

WHAT ELSE TO LOOK FOR?

Apart from the key basic shoes and bags outlined earlier, here are additional suggestions.

Before I begin, remember two things. Firstly, when I talk about jewelry I'm referring to fashion jewelry—stuff that is bold enough and big enough to truly change the look of an outfit. There's always a place for fine jewelry in your outfit, but just remember to mix it up with pieces that are on-trend and, well, just a bit more fun!

Secondly, accessories (especially jewelry) are often a very personal decision, so take my suggestions as simply that—suggestions to inspire your inner stylist to come up with your own magical combination of accessories for your one thousand new looks.

Many of the pieces illustrated here are reflective of pieces I have owned myself. While they may be right for me, they may not be *the* pieces for you.

The idea here is to start seeing the value of accessories and use them to add that 20 percent of icing on the 80 percent vanilla wedding cake. Whether you spend $2 or $200, don't store accessories in that hidden drawer. Love, enjoy, and wear them.

BANGLES AND BRACELETS

I love bangles and bracelets hanging off your wrists as you lift babies from strollers (or lift another drink to your lips—whichever takes your fancy). They always add pizzazz to an outfit.

For the moms of young babies among us, a solid, big bangle is a *great* accessory to dress up your outfit—and it doubles up a great toy, too, when you're absolutely in need of a distraction for your little one.

A classic black bangle (Figure 80) will never go astray. It is able to complement a multitude of outfits. A couple of other options will also jazz up daytime outfits and come in handy a thousand times over.

In these examples, I've selected one in a bright, happy color (Figure 81), a casual earth-toned bangle (Figure 82), and a silver option in case you don't wear gold (Figure 83). Finally, you need a snazzy Sparkling Sally–inspired option for nighttime looks (Figure 84).

FIGURE 80: A basic black bangle

FIGURE 81: A bangle with a shot of color

FIGURE 82: An earth-toned bracelet

FIGURE 83: Choose silver if you don't wear gold

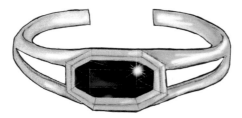

FIGURE 84: A little bling for dressier outfits

NECKLACES

Necklaces are another great choice for fabulous accessories. They're part of what stylists call "eyes-up" accessories, meaning they help draw attention straight to your happy, gorgeous face (detracting from other areas such as hips or tummies).

Start with a basic black necklace (Figure 85) and choose a longer or shorter style depending on what suits you best (as a general rule, very short necklaces may cut you off at the neck, but if you have a very large bustline or tummy, a longer necklace may not sit as well). Make sure it has a bit of "chunk" and weight to it. Since it is black, if it's too dainty, it may get lost in outfits.

I'm also a fan of having a similar necklace but in a color (or colors!) that add real pop to your outfits (Figure 86).

I often suggest a couple of casual necklaces for weekend wear. Usually, this would be a longer style of necklace that will help offset your little tees and tops for the weekend. Shorter necklaces tend to look more constricted and too formal for casual wear.

Figures 87 and 88 illustrate two examples that are my go-to options no matter what the outfit.

FIGURE 85: Necklaces, option 1

FIGURE 86: Necklaces, option 2

FIGURE 87: Necklaces, option 3   **FIGURE 88:** Necklaces, option 4

If you can't find time to accessorize, keep a basic
bangle or necklace hanging with your keys, in the car,
or in your handbag. This way, you'll always have an
accessory within easy reach!

EARRINGS

Earrings are a superstar accessory. Whether big or small, dangly or
petite, a pair of earrings will draw attention straight to the face and
eyes. It is another example of the "eyes-up" accessory.

A casual pair in silver or gold (Figure 89), whichever is your preference, is a terrific starting point. A second pair that has a bit more
sparkle, bling, and general *oomph* is a must for your little black dress

FIGURE 89: Earrings, option 1

FIGURE 90: Earrings, option 2

FIGURE 91: Earrings, option 3

and date nights out. If budget allows, get pairs in both silver or gold (Figure 90, gold in this case) and also one that Sparkling Sally would love in black (Figure 91).

BELTS

Oh belts—how do I heart thee? Let me count the ways and times you have created a waist where no waist has been! Unless you are carrying the bulk of your weight around the tummy area, a belt is a very flattering accessory for almost everyone.

The trick is to ensure that you wear the belt right on your waist—this is often a little higher than what you may be used to—and initially it may feel slightly foreign. You are literally looking for the smallest part of your waist and placing a belt at that point of your body to really emphasize and cinch in that area. This is what creates the illusion of fabulous curves!

(If you have a very short torso, place your belt slightly below your natural waist to create the illusion of length.)

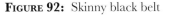

FIGURE 92: Skinny black belt   **FIGURE 93:** Skinny belt in a pop of color

A couple of skinny belts are always versatile and essential in outfits with dresses and pants. Choose belts that will sit around your hips if you are wearing pants. Punch in extra holes if you need to so it can also be worn on your waist. (A shoemaker can do this for you; or if you are a belt junkie like me, you can buy a leather puncher from craft or hardware stores.)

A black version for your staples and another in a bold accent color are all you need to start (Figures 92 and 93).

A belt in cream or white is great for summer looks (try belting it over a stone blazer or with your jeans, rolled up to a crop length). A fancier black belt for black dresses and blazers is a great addition to round out your belt collection (Figures 94 and 95).

FIGURE 94: A white belt   **FIGURE 95:** A sparkly belt for nighttime

SCARVES AND HATS

Whether it's a lightweight scarf for a splash of interest and color in the spring or a pretty yet functional option for winter, scarves are a comforting way to add dimension and depth to your outfit.

A simple print and color (Figure 96) is perfect to finish off any of your simpler outfits in lighter weather, while a colored print (Figure 97) is a fabulous option to inject life and fun into your darker outfits.

Finally, ensure you have a scarf that will keep you cozy in winter, like this faux fur number (Figure 98) in a versatile brown or gray.

FIGURE 96: Scarf, option 1   **FIGURE 97:** Scarf, option 2

FIGURE 98: Scarf, option 3

FIGURE 99: Hat, option 1

FIGURE 100: Hat, option 2

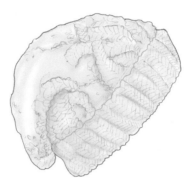

FIGURE 101: Hat, option 3

Hats are an essential if you live somewhere cold. Otherwise, treat it as a fun fashion accessory!

For those in cooler locations, look for winter-style fedoras (Figure 99), as well as a couple more casual options (Figures 100 and 101).

CONCLUDING THE

Capsule Wardrobe

Believe it or not, you now have everything you need for a fabulous wardrobe that will work for you daily.

Whether you're headed to the office, the school run, or hitting the town, you have all the foundational elements you need to look stylish for any occasion. The key to making the capsule wardrobe work for you is to get comfortable with this whole new concept of minimalism.

LET THE TABLE GUIDE YOU

The Appendix on page 122 holds the key to unlocking all one thousand combinations from your thirty capsule wardrobe pieces. In this table, I outline *all* of the combinations I've been able to come up with!

(And, if you extend your capsule with extra items, you'll be able to grow this list and your outfit choices even further!)

This table provides instant access to a thousand looks by combining your thirty pieces in various ways. If you ever feel stuck and unoriginal, just refer to this table.

1. Start with the different bottoms you can choose from (remember: bottoms are our base!). Depending on your occasion, select the bottoms that are most appropriate.
2. Then, move to the right and browse the various tops in the next column.
3. Next, decide whether you will pair a cardigan or jacket with your top to vary the look even more.
4. Continue moving right to find different combinations of shoes and bags that will work with the outfit you've selected.

By using this table as your guide, you can effortlessly make your capsule wardrobe work in any number of ways in a matter of minutes.

As you find combinations that work for you every day, make a note of them.

Highlight your favorites on the table or take a few snapshots of your favorite combinations to refer to in the future.

WHAT NEXT?

As you move forward with this new, streamlined approach to fashion, I have a few final tips to share.

TIP #1—DITCH THE FEAR!

Don't let your fears hold you back from looking chic.

Be *bold* and embrace new combinations. Even if you'd never naturally pair two pieces together, don't let that stop you from at least trying it on.

Ditch the fear and start experimenting with the combinations listed on the table. Try a new look, a new color combination, or a few new accessories.

When you stop living in fashion fear, you start looking fabulous!

TIP #2—FOLLOW THE 80/20 RULE

One of the most important concepts to remember is the 80/20 rule to building a wardrobe. Remember that 80 percent of your wardrobe should come from basics.

This 80 percent will be functional pieces that you can mix and match with a variety of accessories. Once you have the essentials to make up your 80 percent, it's crucial not to ignore the extra touches by adding the 20 percent that will make your wardrobe unique and extraordinarily you!

TIP #3—KNOW WHEN TO LET GO

It's tempting to cling to pieces in your closet that have been around forever. But as you move forward into building a terrific and versatile capsule wardrobe, you need to be willing to let go.

Remember—release the wardrobe clutter, and the mind clutter will follow.

THE MOST IMPORTANT ADDITION TO YOUR CLOSET

As you move forward with your capsule wardrobe, remember the one important addition to your closet:

Confidence!

No matter what your size, shape, or body type, confidence is the key to rocking any wardrobe. With your capsule wardrobe and a confident, seize-the-day attitude, you can conquer the world and feel beautiful every single day.

ENJOY YOUR CAPSULE WARDROBE

Although we've reached the end, this is truly the beginning.

As you start working with your new wardrobe philosophy, I hope you'll see that despite having streamlined your wardrobe, the possibilities grow with each passing day.

Look to create a solid platform, a "blank canvas" of clothing that you can mix and match into a thousand outfits, while balancing that out with pieces you need to add sparkle, life, and interest.

Remember: there's rarely a one-size-fits-all solution to style (as with most things in life), so feel confident enough to adapt what you've learned and make it work for you and your lifestyle.

Begin to look at clothes differently and know that you *can* build a beautiful outfit in moments with just a few basic pieces and accessories. You don't have to spend a fortune on new outfits for every occasion.

All you need is your capsule wardrobe . . . love it and wear it well!

Appendix

	TERRIFIC THIRTY		NOTES AND ALTERNATIVES
	7 bottoms		
1		Jeans	Choose an alternate shape to skinny if that suits you best
2		Casual pant, taupe or mushroom	Look for a casual pant without external pockets or embellishments, such as stitching detail, so you can dress it up if needed
3		Tailored pant, black	Select a style and cut that flatters you best
4		Tailored pant, stone or taupe	Stone or taupe (essentially a few shades darker than your stone jacket) will work best, but you can also select cream, off-white, pale gray, or a very light brown in a more casual fabric than your tailored black pants
5		Tailored shorts	Stone, taupe, or mushroom shorts that are tailored and not too casual in style will enable you to take these from day to night
6		Casual skirt, denim	Although a straight or pencil cut will be the most versatile, select an A-line or a drop waist if these flatter you better
	6 tops		
7		Skirt, black	Look for a skirt that has some detail so it can take you from office to play
8		Basic tank, black	If you aren't a fan of black, select a dark charcoal instead
9		Basic tank, white	If white doesn't suit you, an off-white or cream will do just the trick
10		Blouse, accent color	Choose a bold color that makes you look and feel good, and that works with both black and tan or cream items.
11		Second blouse, accent color	Look to retail stores for color inspiration and, see what's on-trend this season in terms of color
12		Long-sleeved top, accent color	Select a color other than black or white to add additional interest to your wardrobe
13		Long-sleeved top, black	A dark charcoal will also work for those who don't like black
	2 dresses		
14		Casual day dress	Keep any prints or patterns small and congruous, with a mix of light and dark colors in the print for maximum versatility
15		Little black dress	For both work and play; ensure the hem and neckline are modest enough for work, and ideally look for a short or cap sleeve
	6 jackets / outerwear		
16		Coat / trench	A classic coat or trench in a stone or beige will complement everything. If you live in a warmer climate, choose a lighter weight fabric and shorter length coat
17		Cardigan, black	Make sure this gives you plenty of shape; it should not be too baggy or slouchy-looking on you

		NOTES AND ALTERNATIVES
18	Blazer, black	A blazer with a three-quarter sleeve will be easiest to match with jeans, as well as dressier items; it will keep you looking contemporary and young
19	Blazer, stone	Once again, select a three-quarter sleeve; ensure the shade of stone you select is lighter than your casual and tailored pants above
20	Casual jacket	There are many options here in terms of color, so select a color in a relaxed style that will complement your accent-colored blouses
21	Parka, black	Ensure that this is a proper, winter-weight jacket for super cold days; black works best, or choose navy or charcoal if you prefer
22	Everyday tote bag, black	Patent leather will make this tote easy to dress up or down, as the shine adds depth and formality to the bag
23	Everyday tote bag, tan	For maximum versatility, don't go overboard with detailing or hardware on your bags
24	Small clutch, black	If a clutch isn't your thing, a smaller shoulder bag is a great alternative
25	Knee-high boots, black	A pair in patent leather will add pizzazz to any outfit; if you live in a warmer climate, select a small bootie instead
26	Round pumps, black	Once again, patent leather is your friend, taking you from daytime to nighttime in a cinch; a rounded toe is more versatile and easier to match with opaque tights than a pointed toe
27	Wedges, tan	Coordinate the shade of tan to complement your tan tote bag; it doesn't have to be an exact match but it should be a shade in the same color family
28	Strappy heel, black	A t-bar is usually the most flattering style as it elongates your leg and foot
29	Dressy sandals	A flat pair of sandals in tan or bronze will complement your tan tote nicely, and it is much more flattering than rubber flip flops or sneakers
30	Ballet flats, black	Whether you choose patent leather, a croc print, or classic plain leather, you need a comfortable and reliable black ballet flat to run around in

Side labels: 3 bags (rows 22–24), 6 shoes (rows 25–30)

#	TROUSER/ PANT	SKIRT/ SHORTS/ DRESS	TOP	OUTERWEAR	SHOE	BAG
1	Jeans		Basic tank, black		Round pumps, black	Everyday tote bag, black
2	Jeans		Basic tank, black		Round pumps, black	Small clutch, black
3	Jeans		Basic tank, black		Wedges, tan	Everyday tote bag, tan
4	Jeans		Basic tank, black		Ballet flats, black	Everyday tote bag, black
5	Jeans		Basic tank, black		Ballet flats, black	Small clutch, black
6	Jeans		Basic tank, black		Strappy heel, black	Everyday tote bag, black
7	Jeans		Basic tank, black		Strappy heel, black	Small clutch, black
8	Jeans		Basic tank, black		Dressy sandals	Everyday tote bag, tan
9	Jeans		Basic tank, black	Parka / trench coat	Knee-high boots, black	Everyday tote bag, black
10	Jeans		Basic tank, black	Parka / trench coat	Knee-high boots, black	Small clutch, black
11	Jeans		Basic tank, black	Parka / trench coat	Round pumps, black	Everyday tote bag, black
12	Jeans		Basic tank, black	Parka / trench coat	Round pumps, black	Small clutch, black
13	Jeans		Basic tank, black	Parka / trench coat	Wedges, tan	Everyday tote bag, tan
14	Jeans		Basic tank, black	Parka / trench coat	Ballet flats, black	Everyday tote bag, black
15	Jeans		Basic tank, black	Cardigan, black	Knee-high boots, black	Everyday tote bag, black
16	Jeans		Basic tank, black	Cardigan, black	Knee-high boots, black	Small clutch, black
17	Jeans		Basic tank, black	Cardigan, black	Round pumps, black	Everyday tote bag, black
18	Jeans		Basic tank, black	Cardigan, black	Round pumps, black	Small clutch, black
19	Jeans		Basic tank, black	Cardigan, black	Wedges, tan	Everyday tote bag, tan
20	Jeans		Basic tank, black	Cardigan, black	Ballet flats, black	Everyday tote bag, black
21	Jeans		Basic tank, black	Cardigan, black	Ballet flats, black	Small clutch, black
22	Jeans		Basic tank, black	Cardigan, black	Dressy sandals	Everyday tote bag, black
23	Jeans		Basic tank, black	Cardigan, black	Dressy sandals	Everyday tote bag, tan
24	Jeans		Basic tank, black	Cardigan, black	Strappy heel, black	Everyday tote bag, black
25	Jeans		Basic tank, black	Cardigan, black	Strappy heel, black	Small clutch, black
26	Jeans		Basic tank, black	Blazer, black	Knee-high boots, black	Everyday tote bag, black

	TROUSER/ PANT	SKIRT/ SHORTS/ DRESS	TOP	OUTERWEAR	SHOE	BAG
27	Jeans		Basic tank, black	Blazer, black	Knee-high boots, black	Small clutch, black
28	Jeans		Basic tank, black	Blazer, black	Round pumps, black	Everyday tote bag, black
29	Jeans		Basic tank, black	Blazer, black	Round pumps, black	Small clutch, black
30	Jeans		Basic tank, black	Blazer, black	Wedges, tan	Everyday tote bag, tan
31	Jeans		Basic tank, black	Blazer, black	Ballet flats, black	Everyday tote bag, black
32	Jeans		Basic tank, black	Blazer, black	Ballet flats, black	Small clutch, black
33	Jeans		Basic tank, black	Blazer, black	Strappy heel, black	Everyday tote bag, black
34	Jeans		Basic tank, black	Blazer, black	Strappy heel, black	Small clutch, black
35	Jeans		Basic tank, black	Blazer, stone	Knee-high boots, black	Everyday tote bag, black
36	Jeans		Basic tank, black	Blazer, stone	Knee-high boots, black	Everyday tote bag, tan
37	Jeans		Basic tank, black	Blazer, stone	Knee-high boots, black	Small clutch, black
38	Jeans		Basic tank, black	Blazer, stone	Round pumps, black	Everyday tote bag, black
39	Jeans		Basic tank, black	Blazer, stone	Round pumps, black	Everyday tote bag, tan
40	Jeans		Basic tank, black	Blazer, stone	Round pumps, black	Small clutch, black
41	Jeans		Basic tank, black	Blazer, stone	Wedges, tan	Everyday tote bag, tan
42	Jeans		Basic tank, black	Blazer, stone	Ballet flats, black	Everyday tote bag, black
43	Jeans		Basic tank, black	Blazer, stone	Ballet flats, black	Everyday tote bag, tan
44	Jeans		Basic tank, black	Blazer, stone	Ballet flats, black	Small clutch, black
45	Jeans		Basic tank, black	Blazer, stone	Strappy heel, black	Everyday tote bag, black
46	Jeans		Basic tank, black	Blazer, stone	Strappy heel, black	Everyday tote bag, tan
47	Jeans		Basic tank, black	Blazer, stone	Strappy heel, black	Small clutch, black
48	Jeans		Basic tank, black	Casual jacket	Knee-high boots, black	Everyday tote bag, black
49	Jeans		Basic tank, black	Casual jacket	Round pumps, black	Everyday tote bag, black
50	Jeans		Basic tank, black	Casual jacket	Round pumps, black	Small clutch, black
51	Jeans		Basic tank, black	Casual jacket	Wedges, tan	Everyday tote bag, tan
52	Jeans		Basic tank, black	Casual jacket	Ballet flats, black	Everyday tote bag, black

	TROUSER/PANT	SKIRT/SHORTS/DRESS	TOP	OUTERWEAR	SHOE	BAG
53	Jeans		Basic tank, black	Casual jacket	Strappy heel, black	Everyday tote bag, black
54	Jeans		Basic tank, black	Casual jacket	Strappy heel, black	Small clutch, black
55	Jeans		Basic tank, white		Round pumps, black	Everyday tote bag, black
56	Jeans		Basic tank, white		Round pumps, black	Everyday tote bag, tan
57	Jeans		Basic tank, white		Round pumps, black	Small clutch, black
58	Jeans		Basic tank, white		Wedges, tan	Everyday tote bag, tan
59	Jeans		Basic tank, white		Ballet flats, black	Everyday tote bag, black
60	Jeans		Basic tank, white		Ballet flats, black	Everyday tote bag, tan
61	Jeans		Basic tank, white		Strappy heel, black	Everyday tote bag, black
62	Jeans		Basic tank, white		Strappy heel, black	Everyday tote bag, tan
63	Jeans		Basic tank, white		Strappy heel, black	Small clutch, black
64	Jeans		Basic tank, white		Dressy sandals	Everyday tote bag, tan
65	Jeans		Basic tank, white	Parka / trench coat	Knee-high boots, black	Everyday tote bag, black
66	Jeans		Basic tank, white	Parka / trench coat	Knee-high boots, black	Everyday tote bag, tan
67	Jeans		Basic tank, white	Parka / trench coat	Knee-high boots, black	Small clutch, black
68	Jeans		Basic tank, white	Parka / trench coat	Round pumps, black	Everyday tote bag, black
69	Jeans		Basic tank, white	Parka / trench coat	Round pumps, black	Everyday tote bag, tan
70	Jeans		Basic tank, white	Parka / trench coat	Round pumps, black	Small clutch, black
71	Jeans		Basic tank, white	Parka / trench coat	Wedges, tan	Everyday tote bag, tan
72	Jeans		Basic tank, white	Parka / trench coat	Ballet flats, black	Everyday tote bag, black
73	Jeans		Basic tank, white	Parka / trench coat	Ballet flats, black	Everyday tote bag, tan
74	Jeans		Basic tank, white	Cardigan, black	Knee-high boots, black	Everyday tote bag, black
75	Jeans		Basic tank, white	Cardigan, black	Knee-high boots, black	Everyday tote bag, tan
76	Jeans		Basic tank, white	Cardigan, black	Knee-high boots, black	Small clutch, black
77	Jeans		Basic tank, white	Cardigan, black	Round pumps, black	Everyday tote bag, black
78	Jeans		Basic tank, white	Cardigan, black	Round pumps, black	Everyday tote bag, tan
79	Jeans		Basic tank, white	Cardigan, black	Round pumps, black	Small clutch, black
80	Jeans		Basic tank, white	Cardigan, black	Wedges, tan	Everyday tote bag, tan

	TROUSER/PANT	SKIRT/SHORTS/DRESS	TOP	OUTERWEAR	SHOE	BAG
81	Jeans		Basic tank, white	Cardigan, black	Ballet flats, black	Everyday tote bag, black
82	Jeans		Basic tank, white	Cardigan, black	Ballet flats, black	Everyday tote bag, tan
83	Jeans		Basic tank, white	Cardigan, black	Ballet flats, black	Small clutch, black
84	Jeans		Basic tank, white	Cardigan, black	Dressy sandals	Everyday tote bag, black
85	Jeans		Basic tank, white	Cardigan, black	Dressy sandals	Everyday tote bag, tan
86	Jeans		Basic tank, white	Cardigan, black	Strappy heel, black	Everyday tote bag, black
87	Jeans		Basic tank, white	Cardigan, black	Strappy heel, black	Everyday tote bag, tan
88	Jeans		Basic tank, white	Cardigan, black	Strappy heel, black	Small clutch, black
89	Jeans		Basic tank, white	Blazer, black	Knee-high boots, black	Everyday tote bag, black
90	Jeans		Basic tank, white	Blazer, black	Knee-high boots, black	Everyday tote bag, tan
91	Jeans		Basic tank, white	Blazer, black	Knee-high boots, black	Small clutch, black
92	Jeans		Basic tank, white	Blazer, black	Round pumps, black	Everyday tote bag, black
93	Jeans		Basic tank, white	Blazer, black	Round pumps, black	Everyday tote bag, tan
94	Jeans		Basic tank, white	Blazer, black	Round pumps, black	Small clutch, black
95	Jeans		Basic tank, white	Blazer, black	Wedges, tan	Everyday tote bag, tan
96	Jeans		Basic tank, white	Blazer, black	Ballet flats, black	Everyday tote bag, black
97	Jeans		Basic tank, white	Blazer, black	Ballet flats, black	Everyday tote bag, tan
98	Jeans		Basic tank, white	Blazer, black	Ballet flats, black	Small clutch, black
99	Jeans		Basic tank, white	Blazer, black	Strappy heel, black	Everyday tote bag, black
100	Jeans		Basic tank, white	Blazer, black	Strappy heel, black	Everyday tote bag, tan
101	Jeans		Basic tank, white	Blazer, black	Strappy heel, black	Small clutch, black
102	Jeans		Basic tank, white	Blazer, stone	Knee-high boots, black	Everyday tote bag, black
103	Jeans		Basic tank, white	Blazer, stone	Knee-high boots, black	Everyday tote bag, tan
104	Jeans		Basic tank, white	Blazer, stone	Knee-high boots, black	Small clutch, black
105	Jeans		Basic tank, white	Blazer, stone	Round pumps, black	Everyday tote bag, black
106	Jeans		Basic tank, white	Blazer, stone	Round pumps, black	Everyday tote bag, tan
107	Jeans		Basic tank, white	Blazer, stone	Round pumps, black	Small clutch, black
108	Jeans		Basic tank, white	Blazer, stone	Wedges, tan	Everyday tote bag, tan

	TROUSER/PANT	SKIRT/SHORTS/DRESS	TOP	OUTERWEAR	SHOE	BAG
109	Jeans		Basic tank, white	Blazer, stone	Ballet flats, black	Everyday tote bag, black
110	Jeans		Basic tank, white	Blazer, stone	Ballet flats, black	Everyday tote bag, tan
111	Jeans		Basic tank, white	Blazer, stone	Ballet flats, black	Small clutch, black
112	Jeans		Basic tank, white	Blazer, stone	Strappy heel, black	Everyday tote bag, black
113	Jeans		Basic tank, white	Blazer, stone	Strappy heel, black	Everyday tote bag, tan
114	Jeans		Basic tank, white	Blazer, stone	Strappy heel, black	Small clutch, black
115	Jeans		Basic tank, white	Casual jacket	Knee-high boots, black	Everyday tote bag, black
116	Jeans		Basic tank, white	Casual jacket	Knee-high boots, black	Everyday tote bag, tan
117	Jeans		Basic tank, white	Casual jacket	Knee-high boots, black	Small clutch, black
118	Jeans		Basic tank, white	Casual jacket	Round pumps, black	Everyday tote bag, black
119	Jeans		Basic tank, white	Casual jacket	Round pumps, black	Everyday tote bag, tan
120	Jeans		Basic tank, white	Casual jacket	Round pumps, black	Small clutch, black
121	Jeans		Basic tank, white	Casual jacket	Wedges, tan	Everyday tote bag, tan
122	Jeans		Basic tank, white	Casual jacket	Ballet flats, black	Everyday tote bag, black
123	Jeans		Basic tank, white	Casual jacket	Ballet flats, black	Everyday tote bag, tan
124	Jeans		Basic tank, white	Casual jacket	Ballet flats, black	Small clutch, black
125	Jeans		Basic tank, white	Casual jacket	Strappy heel, black	Everyday tote bag, black
126	Jeans		Basic tank, white	Casual jacket	Strappy heel, black	Everyday tote bag, tan
127	Jeans		Basic tank, white	Casual jacket	Strappy heel, black	Small clutch, black
128	Jeans		Blouse, accent color		Round pumps, black	Everyday tote bag, black
129	Jeans		Blouse, accent color		Round pumps, black	Small clutch, black
130	Jeans		Blouse, accent color		Wedges, tan	Everyday tote bag, tan
131	Jeans		Blouse, accent color		Ballet flats, black	Everyday tote bag, black
132	Jeans		Blouse, accent color		Ballet flats, black	Small clutch, black
133	Jeans		Blouse, accent color		Strappy heel, black	Everyday tote bag, black
134	Jeans		Blouse, accent color		Strappy heel, black	Small clutch, black
135	Jeans		Blouse, accent color		Dressy sandals	Everyday tote bag, tan

	TROUSER/ PANT	SKIRT/ SHORTS/ DRESS	TOP	OUTERWEAR	SHOE	BAG
136	Jeans		Blouse, accent color	Parka / trench coat	Knee-high boots, black	Everyday tote bag, black
137	Jeans		Blouse, accent color	Parka / trench coat	Knee-high boots, black	Small clutch, black
138	Jeans		Blouse, accent color	Parka / trench coat	Round pumps, black	Everyday tote bag, black
139	Jeans		Blouse, accent color	Parka / trench coat	Round pumps, black	Small clutch, black
140	Jeans		Blouse, accent color	Parka / trench coat	Wedges, tan	Everyday tote bag, tan
141	Jeans		Blouse, accent color	Parka / trench coat	Ballet flats, black	Everyday tote bag, black
142	Jeans		Blouse, accent color	Parka / trench coat	Ballet flats, black	Small clutch, black
143	Jeans		Blouse, accent color	Cardigan, black	Knee-high boots, black	Everyday tote bag, black
144	Jeans		Blouse, accent color	Cardigan, black	Knee-high boots, black	Small clutch, black
145	Jeans		Blouse, accent color	Cardigan, black	Round pumps, black	Everyday tote bag, black
146	Jeans		Blouse, accent color	Cardigan, black	Round pumps, black	Small clutch, black
147	Jeans		Blouse, accent color	Cardigan, black	Wedges, tan	Everyday tote bag, tan
148	Jeans		Blouse, accent color	Cardigan, black	Ballet flats, black	Everyday tote bag, black
149	Jeans		Blouse, accent color	Cardigan, black	Ballet flats, black	Small clutch, black
150	Jeans		Blouse, accent color	Cardigan, black	Dressy sandals	Everyday tote bag, black
151	Jeans		Blouse, accent color	Cardigan, black	Dressy sandals	Everyday tote bag, tan
152	Jeans		Blouse, accent color	Cardigan, black	Strappy heel, black	Everyday tote bag, black
153	Jeans		Blouse, accent color	Cardigan, black	Strappy heel, black	Small clutch, black
154	Jeans		Blouse, accent color	Blazer, black	Knee-high boots, black	Everyday tote bag, black
155	Jeans		Blouse, accent color	Blazer, black	Knee-high boots, black	Everyday tote bag, tan
156	Jeans		Blouse, accent color	Blazer, black	Knee-high boots, black	Small clutch, black
157	Jeans		Blouse, accent color	Blazer, black	Round pumps, black	Everyday tote bag, black
158	Jeans		Blouse, accent color	Blazer, black	Round pumps, black	Small clutch, black
159	Jeans		Blouse, accent color	Blazer, black	Wedges, tan	Everyday tote bag, tan
160	Jeans		Blouse, accent color	Blazer, black	Ballet flats, black	Everyday tote bag, black
161	Jeans		Blouse, accent color	Blazer, black	Ballet flats, black	Small clutch, black
162	Jeans		Blouse, accent color	Blazer, black	Strappy heel, black	Everyday tote bag, black

	TROUSER/PANT	SKIRT/SHORTS/DRESS	TOP	OUTERWEAR	SHOE	BAG
163	Jeans		Blouse, accent color	Blazer, black	Strappy heel, black	Small clutch, black
164	Jeans		Blouse, accent color	Blazer, stone	Knee-high boots, black	Everyday tote bag, black
165	Jeans		Blouse, accent color	Blazer, stone	Knee-high boots, black	Everyday tote bag, tan
166	Jeans		Blouse, accent color	Blazer, stone	Knee-high boots, black	Small clutch, black
167	Jeans		Blouse, accent color	Blazer, stone	Round pumps, black	Everyday tote bag, black
168	Jeans		Blouse, accent color	Blazer, stone	Round pumps, black	Everyday tote bag, tan
169	Jeans		Blouse, accent color	Blazer, stone	Round pumps, black	Small clutch, black
170	Jeans		Blouse, accent color	Blazer, stone	Wedges, tan	Everyday tote bag, tan
171	Jeans		Blouse, accent color	Blazer, stone	Ballet flats, black	Everyday tote bag, black
172	Jeans		Blouse, accent color	Blazer, stone	Ballet flats, black	Everyday tote bag, tan
173	Jeans		Blouse, accent color	Blazer, stone	Ballet flats, black	Small clutch, black
174	Jeans		Blouse, accent color	Blazer, stone	Strappy heel, black	Everyday tote bag, black
175	Jeans		Blouse, accent color	Blazer, stone	Strappy heel, black	Everyday tote bag, tan
176	Jeans		Blouse, accent color	Blazer, stone	Strappy heel, black	Small clutch, black
177	Jeans		Blouse, accent color	Casual jacket	Knee-high boots, black	Everyday tote bag, black
178	Jeans		Blouse, accent color	Casual jacket	Knee-high boots, black	Everyday tote bag, tan
179	Jeans		Blouse, accent color	Casual jacket	Knee-high boots, black	Small clutch, black
180	Jeans		Blouse, accent color	Casual jacket	Round pumps, black	Everyday tote bag, black
181	Jeans		Blouse, accent color	Casual jacket	Round pumps, black	Everyday tote bag, tan
182	Jeans		Blouse, accent color	Casual jacket	Round pumps, black	Small clutch, black
183	Jeans		Blouse, accent color	Casual jacket	Wedges, tan	Everyday tote bag, tan
184	Jeans		Blouse, accent color	Casual jacket	Ballet flats, black	Everyday tote bag, black
185	Jeans		Blouse, accent color	Casual jacket	Ballet flats, black	Everyday tote bag, tan
186	Jeans		Blouse, accent color	Casual jacket	Ballet flats, black	Small clutch, black
187	Jeans		Blouse, accent color	Casual jacket	Strappy heel, black	Everyday tote bag, black
188	Jeans		Blouse, accent color	Casual jacket	Strappy heel, black	Everyday tote bag, tan
189	Jeans		Blouse, accent color	Casual jacket	Strappy heel, black	Small clutch, black
190	Jeans		Blouse, accent color	Casual jacket	Dressy sandals	Everyday tote bag, tan

	TROUSER/ PANT	SKIRT/ SHORTS/ DRESS	TOP	OUTERWEAR	SHOE	BAG
191	Jeans		Second blouse, accent color		Round pumps, black	Everyday tote bag, black
192	Jeans		Second blouse, accent color		Round pumps, black	Small clutch, black
193	Jeans		Second blouse, accent color		Wedges, tan	Everyday tote bag, tan
194	Jeans		Second blouse, accent color		Ballet flats, black	Everyday tote bag, black
195	Jeans		Second blouse, accent color		Ballet flats, black	Small clutch, black
196	Jeans		Second blouse, accent color		Strappy heel, black	Everyday tote bag, black
197	Jeans		Second blouse, accent color		Strappy heel, black	Small clutch, black
198	Jeans		Second blouse, accent color		Dressy sandals	Everyday tote bag, tan
199	Jeans		Second blouse, accent color	Parka / trench coat	Knee-high boots, black	Everyday tote bag, black
200	Jeans		Second blouse, accent color	Parka / trench coat	Knee-high boots, black	Small clutch, black
201	Jeans		Second blouse, accent color	Parka / trench coat	Round pumps, black	Everyday tote bag, black
202	Jeans		Second blouse, accent color	Parka / trench coat	Round pumps, black	Small clutch, black
203	Jeans		Second blouse, accent color	Parka / trench coat	Wedges, tan	Everyday tote bag, tan
204	Jeans		Second blouse, accent color	Parka / trench coat	Ballet flats, black	Everyday tote bag, black
205	Jeans		Second blouse, accent color	Parka / trench coat	Ballet flats, black	Small clutch, black
206	Jeans		Second blouse, accent color	Cardigan, black	Knee-high boots, black	Everyday tote bag, black
207	Jeans		Second blouse, accent color	Cardigan, black	Knee-high boots, black	Small clutch, black
208	Jeans		Second blouse, accent color	Cardigan, black	Round pumps, black	Everyday tote bag, black
209	Jeans		Second blouse, accent color	Cardigan, black	Round pumps, black	Small clutch, black
210	Jeans		Second blouse, accent color	Cardigan, black	Wedges, tan	Everyday tote bag, tan
211	Jeans		Second blouse, accent color	Cardigan, black	Ballet flats, black	Everyday tote bag, black
212	Jeans		Second blouse, accent color	Cardigan, black	Ballet flats, black	Small clutch, black
213	Jeans		Second blouse, accent color	Cardigan, black	Dressy sandals	Everyday tote bag, black
214	Jeans		Second blouse, accent color	Cardigan, black	Dressy sandals	Everyday tote bag, tan
215	Jeans		Second blouse, accent color	Cardigan, black	Strappy heel, black	Everyday tote bag, black
216	Jeans		Second blouse, accent color	Cardigan, black	Strappy heel, black	Small clutch, black
217	Jeans		Second blouse, accent color	Blazer, black	Knee-high boots, black	Everyday tote bag, black

	TROUSER/PANT	SKIRT/SHORTS/DRESS	TOP	OUTERWEAR	SHOE	BAG
218	Jeans		Second blouse, accent color	Blazer, black	Knee-high boots, black	Small clutch, black
219	Jeans		Second blouse, accent color	Blazer, black	Round pumps, black	Everyday tote bag, black
220	Jeans		Second blouse, accent color	Blazer, black	Round pumps, black	Small clutch, black
221	Jeans		Second blouse, accent color	Blazer, black	Wedges, tan	Everyday tote bag, tan
222	Jeans		Second blouse, accent color	Blazer, black	Ballet flats, black	Everyday tote bag, black
223	Jeans		Second blouse, accent color	Blazer, black	Ballet flats, black	Small clutch, black
224	Jeans		Second blouse, accent color	Blazer, black	Strappy heel, black	Everyday tote bag, black
225	Jeans		Second blouse, accent color	Blazer, black	Strappy heel, black	Small clutch, black
226	Jeans		Second blouse, accent color	Blazer, stone	Knee-high boots, black	Everyday tote bag, black
227	Jeans		Second blouse, accent color	Blazer, stone	Knee-high boots, black	Everyday tote bag, tan
228	Jeans		Second blouse, accent color	Blazer, stone	Knee-high boots, black	Small clutch, black
229	Jeans		Second blouse, accent color	Blazer, stone	Round pumps, black	Everyday tote bag, black
230	Jeans		Second blouse, accent color	Blazer, stone	Round pumps, black	Everyday tote bag, tan
231	Jeans		Second blouse, accent color	Blazer, stone	Round pumps, black	Small clutch, black
232	Jeans		Second blouse, accent color	Blazer, stone	Wedges, tan	Everyday tote bag, tan
233	Jeans		Second blouse, accent color	Blazer, stone	Ballet flats, black	Everyday tote bag, black
234	Jeans		Second blouse, accent color	Blazer, stone	Ballet flats, black	Everyday tote bag, tan
235	Jeans		Second blouse, accent color	Blazer, stone	Ballet flats, black	Small clutch, black
236	Jeans		Second blouse, accent color	Blazer, stone	Strappy heel, black	Everyday tote bag, black
237	Jeans		Second blouse, accent color	Blazer, stone	Strappy heel, black	Everyday tote bag, tan
238	Jeans		Second blouse, accent color	Blazer, stone	Strappy heel, black	Small clutch, black
239	Jeans		Second blouse, accent color	Casual jacket	Knee-high boots, black	Everyday tote bag, black
240	Jeans		Second blouse, accent color	Casual jacket	Knee-high boots, black	Everyday tote bag, tan
241	Jeans		Second blouse, accent color	Casual jacket	Knee-high boots, black	Small clutch, black
242	Jeans		Second blouse, accent color	Casual jacket	Round pumps, black	Everyday tote bag, black
243	Jeans		Second blouse, accent color	Casual jacket	Round pumps, black	Everyday tote bag, tan
244	Jeans		Second blouse, accent color	Casual jacket	Round pumps, black	Small clutch, black

	TROUSER/PANT	SKIRT/SHORTS/DRESS	TOP	OUTERWEAR	SHOE	BAG
245	Jeans		Second blouse, accent color	Casual jacket	Wedges, tan	Everyday tote bag, tan
246	Jeans		Second blouse, accent color	Casual jacket	Ballet flats, black	Everyday tote bag, black
247	Jeans		Second blouse, accent color	Casual jacket	Ballet flats, black	Everyday tote bag, tan
248	Jeans		Second blouse, accent color	Casual jacket	Ballet flats, black	Small clutch, black
249	Jeans		Second blouse, accent color	Casual jacket	Strappy heel, black	Everyday tote bag, black
250	Jeans		Second blouse, accent color	Casual jacket	Strappy heel, black	Everyday tote bag, tan
251	Jeans		Second blouse, accent color	Casual jacket	Strappy heel, black	Small clutch, black
252	Jeans		Second blouse, accent color	Casual jacket	Dressy sandals	Everyday tote bag, tan
253	Jeans		Three-quarter sleeved top, black		Round pumps, black	Everyday tote bag, black
254	Jeans		Three-quarter sleeved top, black		Round pumps, black	Small clutch, black
255	Jeans		Three-quarter sleeved top, black		Strappy heel, black	Small clutch, black
256	Jeans		Three-quarter sleeved top, black		Dressy sandals	Everyday tote bag, tan
257	Jeans		Three-quarter sleeved top, black		Wedges, tan	Everyday tote bag, tan
258	Jeans		Three-quarter sleeved top, black		Ballet flats, black	Everyday tote bag, black
259	Jeans		Three-quarter sleeved top, black		Ballet flats, black	Small clutch, black
260	Jeans		Three-quarter sleeved top, black	Parka / trench coat	Knee-high boots, black	Everyday tote bag, black
261	Jeans		Three-quarter sleeved top, black	Parka / trench coat	Knee-high boots, black	Small clutch, black
262	Jeans		Three-quarter sleeved top, black	Parka / trench coat	Round pumps, black	Everyday tote bag, black
263	Jeans		Three-quarter sleeved top, black	Parka / trench coat	Round pumps, black	Small clutch, black

	TROUSER/ PANT	SKIRT/ SHORTS/ DRESS	TOP	OUTERWEAR	SHOE	BAG
264	Jeans		Three-quarter sleeved top, black	Parka / trench coat	Wedges, tan	Everyday tote bag, tan
265	Jeans		Three-quarter sleeved top, black	Parka / trench coat	Ballet flats, black	Everyday tote bag, black
266	Jeans		Three-quarter sleeved top, black	Parka / trench coat	Ballet flats, black	Small clutch, black
267	Jeans		Three-quarter sleeved top, black	Cardigan, black	Knee-high boots, black	Everyday tote bag, black
268	Jeans		Three-quarter sleeved top, black	Cardigan, black	Knee-high boots, black	Small clutch, black
269	Jeans		Three-quarter sleeved top, black	Cardigan, black	Round pumps, black	Everyday tote bag, black
270	Jeans		Three-quarter sleeved top, black	Cardigan, black	Round pumps, black	Small clutch, black
271	Jeans		Three-quarter sleeved top, black	Cardigan, black	Wedges, tan	Everyday tote bag, tan
272	Jeans		Three-quarter sleeved top, black	Cardigan, black	Ballet flats, black	Everyday tote bag, black
273	Jeans		Three-quarter sleeved top, black	Cardigan, black	Ballet flats, black	Small clutch, black
274	Jeans		Three-quarter sleeved top, black	Cardigan, black	Dressy sandals	Everyday tote bag, black
275	Jeans		Three-quarter sleeved top, black	Cardigan, black	Dressy sandals	Everyday tote bag, tan
276	Jeans		Three-quarter sleeved top, black	Cardigan, black	Strappy heel, black	Everyday tote bag, black
277	Jeans		Three-quarter sleeved top, black	Cardigan, black	Strappy heel, black	Small clutch, black
278	Jeans		Three-quarter sleeved top, black	Blazer, black	Knee-high boots, black	Everyday tote bag, black
279	Jeans		Three-quarter sleeved top, black	Blazer, black	Knee-high boots, black	Small clutch, black

	TROUSER/ PANT	SKIRT/ SHORTS/ DRESS	TOP	OUTERWEAR	SHOE	BAG
280	Jeans		Three-quarter sleeved top, black	Blazer, black	Round pumps, black	Everyday tote bag, black
281	Jeans		Three-quarter sleeved top, black	Blazer, black	Round pumps, black	Small clutch, black
282	Jeans		Three-quarter sleeved top, black	Blazer, black	Wedges, tan	Everyday tote bag, tan
283	Jeans		Three-quarter sleeved top, black	Blazer, black	Ballet flats, black	Everyday tote bag, black
284	Jeans		Three-quarter sleeved top, black	Blazer, black	Ballet flats, black	Small clutch, black
285	Jeans		Three-quarter sleeved top, black	Blazer, black	Strappy heel, black	Everyday tote bag, black
286	Jeans		Three-quarter sleeved top, black	Blazer, black	Strappy heel, black	Small clutch, black
287	Jeans		Three-quarter sleeved top, black	Blazer, stone	Knee-high boots, black	Everyday tote bag, black
288	Jeans		Three-quarter sleeved top, black	Blazer, stone	Knee-high boots, black	Everyday tote bag, tan
289	Jeans		Three-quarter sleeved top, black	Blazer, stone	Knee-high boots, black	Small clutch, black
290	Jeans		Three-quarter sleeved top, black	Blazer, stone	Round pumps, black	Everyday tote bag, black
291	Jeans		Three-quarter sleeved top, black	Blazer, stone	Round pumps, black	Everyday tote bag, tan
292	Jeans		Three-quarter sleeved top, black	Blazer, stone	Round pumps, black	Small clutch, black
293	Jeans		Three-quarter sleeved top, black	Blazer, stone	Wedges, tan	Everyday tote bag, tan
294	Jeans		Three-quarter sleeved top, black	Blazer, stone	Ballet flats, black	Everyday tote bag, black

	TROUSER/PANT	SKIRT/SHORTS/DRESS	TOP	OUTERWEAR	SHOE	BAG
295	Jeans		Three-quarter sleeved top, black	Blazer, stone	Ballet flats, black	Everyday tote bag, tan
296	Jeans		Three-quarter sleeved top, black	Blazer, stone	Ballet flats, black	Small clutch, black
297	Jeans		Three-quarter sleeved top, black	Blazer, stone	Strappy heel, black	Everyday tote bag, black
298	Jeans		Three-quarter sleeved top, black	Blazer, stone	Strappy heel, black	Everyday tote bag, tan
299	Jeans		Three-quarter sleeved top, black	Blazer, stone	Strappy heel, black	Small clutch, black
300	Jeans		Three-quarter sleeved top, black	Casual jacket	Knee-high boots, black	Everyday tote bag, black
301	Jeans		Three-quarter sleeved top, black	Casual jacket	Knee-high boots, black	Everyday tote bag, tan
302	Jeans		Three-quarter sleeved top, black	Casual jacket	Knee-high boots, black	Small clutch, black
303	Jeans		Three-quarter sleeved top, black	Casual jacket	Round pumps, black	Everyday tote bag, black
304	Jeans		Three-quarter sleeved top, black	Casual jacket	Round pumps, black	Everyday tote bag, tan
305	Jeans		Three-quarter sleeved top, black	Casual jacket	Round pumps, black	Small clutch, black
306	Jeans		Three-quarter sleeved top, black	Casual jacket	Wedges, tan	Everyday tote bag, tan
307	Jeans		Three-quarter sleeved top, black	Casual jacket	Ballet flats, black	Everyday tote bag, black
308	Jeans		Three-quarter sleeved top, black	Casual jacket	Ballet flats, black	Everyday tote bag, tan
309	Jeans		Three-quarter sleeved top, black	Casual jacket	Ballet flats, black	Small clutch, black
310	Jeans		Three-quarter sleeved top, black	Casual jacket	Strappy heel, black	Everyday tote bag, black

	TROUSER/ PANT	SKIRT/ SHORTS/ DRESS	TOP	OUTERWEAR	SHOE	BAG
311	Jeans		Three-quarter sleeved top, black	Casual jacket	Strappy heel, black	Everyday tote bag, tan
312	Jeans		Three-quarter sleeved top, black	Casual jacket	Strappy heel, black	Small clutch, black
313	Jeans		Three-quarter sleeved top, black	Casual jacket	Dressy sandals	Everyday tote bag, tan
314	Jeans		Three-quarter sleeved top, accent color		Round pumps, black	Everyday tote bag, black
315	Jeans		Three-quarter sleeved top, accent color		Round pumps, black	Small clutch, black
316	Jeans		Three-quarter sleeved top, accent color		Strappy heel, black	Small clutch, black
317	Jeans		Three-quarter sleeved top, accent color		Dressy sandals	Everyday tote bag, tan
318	Jeans		Three-quarter sleeved top, accent color		Wedges, tan	Everyday tote bag, tan
319	Jeans		Three-quarter sleeved top, accent color		Ballet flats, black	Everyday tote bag, black
320	Jeans		Three-quarter sleeved top, accent color		Ballet flats, black	Small clutch, black
321	Jeans		Three-quarter sleeved top, accent color	Parka / trench coat	Knee-high boots, black	Everyday tote bag, black
322	Jeans		Three-quarter sleeved top, accent color	Parka / trench coat	Round pumps, black	Everyday tote bag, black
323	Jeans		Three-quarter sleeved top, accent color	Parka / trench coat	Round pumps, black	Small clutch, black
324	Jeans		Three-quarter sleeved top, accent color	Parka / trench coat	Wedges, tan	Everyday tote bag, tan
325	Jeans		Three-quarter sleeved top, accent color	Parka / trench coat	Ballet flats, black	Everyday tote bag, black

	TROUSER/PANT	SKIRT/SHORTS/DRESS	TOP	OUTERWEAR	SHOE	BAG
326	Jeans		Three-quarter sleeved top, accent color	Cardigan, black	Knee-high boots, black	Everyday tote bag, black
327	Jeans		Three-quarter sleeved top, accent color	Cardigan, black	Knee-high boots, black	Small clutch, black
328	Jeans		Three-quarter sleeved top, accent color	Cardigan, black	Round pumps, black	Everyday tote bag, black
329	Jeans		Three-quarter sleeved top, accent color	Cardigan, black	Round pumps, black	Small clutch, black
330	Jeans		Three-quarter sleeved top, accent color	Cardigan, black	Wedges, tan	Everyday tote bag, tan
331	Jeans		Three-quarter sleeved top, accent color	Cardigan, black	Ballet flats, black	Everyday tote bag, black
332	Jeans		Three-quarter sleeved top, accent color	Cardigan, black	Ballet flats, black	Small clutch, black
333	Jeans		Three-quarter sleeved top, accent color	Cardigan, black	Dressy sandals	Everyday tote bag, black
334	Jeans		Three-quarter sleeved top, accent color	Cardigan, black	Dressy sandals	Everyday tote bag, tan
335	Jeans		Three-quarter sleeved top, accent color	Cardigan, black	Strappy heel, black	Everyday tote bag, black
336	Jeans		Three-quarter sleeved top, accent color	Cardigan, black	Strappy heel, black	Small clutch, black
337	Jeans		Three-quarter sleeved top, accent color	Blazer, black	Knee-high boots, black	Everyday tote bag, black
338	Jeans		Three-quarter sleeved top, accent color	Blazer, black	Knee-high boots, black	Small clutch, black
339	Jeans		Three-quarter sleeved top, accent color	Blazer, black	Round pumps, black	Everyday tote bag, black
340	Jeans		Three-quarter sleeved top, accent color	Blazer, black	Round pumps, black	Small clutch, black
341	Jeans		Three-quarter sleeved top, accent color	Blazer, black	Wedges, tan	Everyday tote bag, tan

	TROUSER/ PANT	SKIRT/ SHORTS/ DRESS	TOP	OUTERWEAR	SHOE	BAG
342	Jeans		Three-quarter sleeved top, accent color	Blazer, black	Ballet flats, black	Everyday tote bag, black
343	Jeans		Three-quarter sleeved top, accent color	Blazer, black	Ballet flats, black	Small clutch, black
344	Jeans		Three-quarter sleeved top, accent color	Blazer, black	Strappy heel, black	Everyday tote bag, black
345	Jeans		Three-quarter sleeved top, accent color	Blazer, black	Strappy heel, black	Small clutch, black
346	Jeans		Three-quarter sleeved top, accent color	Blazer, stone	Knee-high boots, black	Everyday tote bag, black
347	Jeans		Three-quarter sleeved top, accent color	Blazer, stone	Knee-high boots, black	Everyday tote bag, tan
348	Jeans		Three-quarter sleeved top, accent color	Blazer, stone	Knee-high boots, black	Small clutch, black
349	Jeans		Three-quarter sleeved top, accent color	Blazer, stone	Round pumps, black	Everyday tote bag, black
350	Jeans		Three-quarter sleeved top, accent color	Blazer, stone	Round pumps, black	Everyday tote bag, tan
351	Jeans		Three-quarter sleeved top, accent color	Blazer, stone	Round pumps, black	Small clutch, black
352	Jeans		Three-quarter sleeved top, accent color	Blazer, stone	Wedges, tan	Everyday tote bag, tan
353	Jeans		Three-quarter sleeved top, accent color	Blazer, stone	Ballet flats, black	Everyday tote bag, black
354	Jeans		Three-quarter sleeved top, accent color	Blazer, stone	Ballet flats, black	Everyday tote bag, tan
355	Jeans		Three-quarter sleeved top, accent color	Blazer, stone	Ballet flats, black	Small clutch, black
356	Jeans		Three-quarter sleeved top, accent color	Blazer, stone	Strappy heel, black	Everyday tote bag, black

	TROUSER/ PANT	SKIRT/ SHORTS/ DRESS	TOP	OUTERWEAR	SHOE	BAG
357	Jeans		Three-quarter sleeved top, accent color	Blazer, stone	Strappy heel, black	Everyday tote bag, tan
358	Jeans		Three-quarter sleeved top, accent color	Blazer, stone	Strappy heel, black	Small clutch, black
359	Jeans		Three-quarter sleeved top, accent color	Casual jacket	Knee-high boots, black	Everyday tote bag, black
360	Jeans		Three-quarter sleeved top, accent color	Casual jacket	Knee-high boots, black	Everyday tote bag, tan
361	Jeans		Three-quarter sleeved top, accent color	Casual jacket	Knee-high boots, black	Small clutch, black
362	Jeans		Three-quarter sleeved top, accent color	Casual jacket	Round pumps, black	Everyday tote bag, black
363	Jeans		Three-quarter sleeved top, accent color	Casual jacket	Round pumps, black	Everyday tote bag, tan
364	Jeans		Three-quarter sleeved top, accent color	Casual jacket	Round pumps, black	Small clutch, black
365	Jeans		Three-quarter sleeved top, accent color	Casual jacket	Wedges, tan	Everyday tote bag, tan
366	Jeans		Three-quarter sleeved top, wwaccent color	Casual jacket	Ballet flats, black	Everyday tote bag, black
367	Jeans		Three-quarter sleeved top, accent color	Casual jacket	Ballet flats, black	Everyday tote bag, tan
368	Jeans		Three-quarter sleeved top, accent color	Casual jacket	Ballet flats, black	Small clutch, black
369	Jeans		Three-quarter sleeved top, accent color	Casual jacket	Strappy heel, black	Everyday tote bag, black
370	Jeans		Three-quarter sleeved top, accent color	Casual jacket	Strappy heel, black	Everyday tote bag, tan
371	Jeans		Three-quarter sleeved top, accent color	Casual jacket	Strappy heel, black	Small clutch, black
372	Jeans		Three-quarter sleeved top, accent color	Casual jacket	Dressy sandals	Everyday tote bag, tan

	TROUSER/ PANT	SKIRT/ SHORTS/ DRESS	TOP	OUTERWEAR	SHOE	BAG
373	Casual pant, taupe or mushroom		Basic tank, black		Round pumps, black	Everyday tote bag, black
374	Casual pant, taupe or mushroom		Basic tank, black		Round pumps, black	Small clutch, black
375	Casual pant, taupe or mushroom		Basic tank, black		Ballet flats, black	Everyday tote bag, black
376	Casual pant, taupe or mushroom		Basic tank, black		Ballet flats, black	Small clutch, black
377	Casual pant, taupe or mushroom		Basic tank, black		Dressy sandals	Everyday tote bag, tan
378	Casual pant, taupe or mushroom		Basic tank, black		Wedges, tan	Everyday tote bag, tan
379	Casual pant, taupe or mushroom		Basic tank, black	Parka / trench coat	Round pumps, black	Everyday tote bag, black
380	Casual pant, taupe or mushroom		Basic tank, black	Parka / trench coat	Round pumps, black	Small clutch, black
381	Casual pant, taupe or mushroom		Basic tank, black	Parka / trench coat	Ballet flats, black	Everyday tote bag, black
382	Casual pant, taupe or mushroom		Basic tank, black	Parka / trench coat	Ballet flats, black	Small clutch, black

	TROUSER/ PANT	SKIRT/ SHORTS/ DRESS	TOP	OUTERWEAR	SHOE	BAG
383	Casual pant, taupe or mushroom		Basic tank, black	Cardigan, black	Round pumps, black	Everyday tote bag, black
384	Casual pant, taupe or mushroom		Basic tank, black	Cardigan, black	Round pumps, black	Small clutch, black
385	Casual pant, taupe or mushroom		Basic tank, black	Cardigan, black	Ballet flats, black	Everyday tote bag, black
386	Casual pant, taupe or mushroom		Basic tank, black	Cardigan, black	Ballet flats, black	Small clutch, black
387	Casual pant, taupe or mushroom		Basic tank, black	Cardigan, black	Dressy sandals	Everyday tote bag, tan
388	Casual pant, taupe or mushroom		Basic tank, black	Cardigan, black	Wedges, tan	Everyday tote bag, tan
389	Casual pant, taupe or mushroom		Basic tank, black	Casual jacket	Wedges, tan	Everyday tote bag, tan
390	Casual pant, taupe or mushroom		Basic tank, black	Casual jacket	Ballet flats, black	Everyday tote bag, black
391	Casual pant, taupe or mushroom		Basic tank, black	Casual jacket	Dressy sandals	Everyday tote bag, tan
392	Casual pant, taupe or mushroom		Basic tank, white		Round pumps, black	Everyday tote bag, black
393	Casual pant, taupe or mushroom		Basic tank, white		Round pumps, black	Small clutch, black

	TROUSER/ PANT	SKIRT/ SHORTS/ DRESS	TOP	OUTERWEAR	SHOE	BAG
394	Casual pant, taupe or mushroom		Basic tank, white		Ballet flats, black	Everyday tote bag, black
395	Casual pant, taupe or mushroom		Basic tank, white		Ballet flats, black	Small clutch, black
396	Casual pant, taupe or mushroom		Basic tank, white		Dressy sandals	Everyday tote bag, tan
397	Casual pant, taupe or mushroom		Basic tank, white		Wedges, tan	Everyday tote bag, tan
398	Casual pant, taupe or mushroom		Basic tank, white	Parka / trench coat	Round pumps, black	Everyday tote bag, black
399	Casual pant, taupe or mushroom		Basic tank, white	Parka / trench coat	Round pumps, black	Small clutch, black
400	Casual pant, taupe or mushroom		Basic tank, white	Parka / trench coat	Ballet flats, black	Everyday tote bag, black
401	Casual pant, taupe or mushroom		Basic tank, white	Parka / trench coat	Ballet flats, black	Small clutch, black
402	Casual pant, taupe or mushroom		Basic tank, white	Cardigan, black	Round pumps, black	Everyday tote bag, black
403	Casual pant, taupe or mushroom		Basic tank, white	Cardigan, black	Round pumps, black	Everyday tote bag, tan

	TROUSER/ PANT	SKIRT/ SHORTS/ DRESS	TOP	OUTERWEAR	SHOE	BAG
404	Casual pant, taupe or mushroom		Basic tank, white	Cardigan, black	Round pumps, black	Small clutch, black
405	Casual pant, taupe or mushroom		Basic tank, white	Cardigan, black	Ballet flats, black	Everyday tote bag, black
406	Casual pant, taupe or mushroom		Basic tank, white	Cardigan, black	Ballet flats, black	Everyday tote bag, tan
407	Casual pant, taupe or mushroom		Basic tank, white	Cardigan, black	Ballet flats, black	Small clutch, black
408	Casual pant, taupe or mushroom		Basic tank, white	Cardigan, black	Dressy sandals	Everyday tote bag, black
409	Casual pant, taupe or mushroom		Basic tank, white	Cardigan, black	Dressy sandals	Everyday tote bag, tan
410	Casual pant, taupe or mushroom		Basic tank, white	Cardigan, black	Dressy sandals	Small clutch, black
411	Casual pant, taupe or mushroom		Basic tank, white	Cardigan, black	Wedges, tan	Everyday tote bag, tan
412	Casual pant, taupe or mushroom		Basic tank, white	Cardigan, black	Wedges, tan	Everyday tote bag, black
413	Casual pant, taupe or mushroom		Basic tank, white	Casual jacket	Round pumps, black	Everyday tote bag, black
414	Casual pant, taupe or mushroom		Basic tank, white	Casual jacket	Round pumps, black	Everyday tote bag, tan

	TROUSER/ PANT	SKIRT/ SHORTS/ DRESS	TOP	OUTERWEAR	SHOE	BAG
415	Casual pant, taupe or mushroom		Basic tank, white	Casual jacket	Round pumps, black	Small clutch, black
416	Casual pant, taupe or mushroom		Basic tank, white	Casual jacket	Ballet flats, black	Everyday tote bag, black
417	Casual pant, taupe or mushroom		Basic tank, white	Casual jacket	Ballet flats, black	Everyday tote bag, tan
418	Casual pant, taupe or mushroom		Basic tank, white	Casual jacket	Ballet flats, black	Small clutch, black
419	Casual pant, taupe or mushroom		Basic tank, white	Casual jacket	Dressy sandals	Everyday tote bag, black
420	Casual pant, taupe or mushroom		Basic tank, white	Casual jacket	Dressy sandals	Everyday tote bag, tan
421	Casual pant, taupe or mushroom		Basic tank, white	Casual jacket	Dressy sandals	Small clutch, black
422	Casual pant, taupe or mushroom		Basic tank, white	Casual jacket	Wedges, tan	Everyday tote bag, tan
423	Casual pant, taupe or mushroom		Basic tank, white	Casual jacket	Wedges, tan	Everyday tote bag, black
424	Casual pant, taupe or mushroom		Blouse, accent color		Round pumps, black	Everyday tote bag, black

	TROUSER/ PANT	SKIRT/ SHORTS/ DRESS	TOP	OUTERWEAR	SHOE	BAG
425	Casual pant, taupe or mushroom		Blouse, accent color		Round pumps, black	Small clutch, black
426	Casual pant, taupe or mushroom		Blouse, accent color		Ballet flats, black	Everyday tote bag, black
427	Casual pant, taupe or mushroom		Blouse, accent color		Ballet flats, black	Small clutch, black
428	Casual pant, taupe or mushroom		Blouse, accent color		Dressy sandals	Everyday tote bag, tan
429	Casual pant, taupe or mushroom		Blouse, accent color		Wedges, tan	Everyday tote bag, tan
430	Casual pant, taupe or mushroom		Blouse, accent color	Parka / trench coat	Round pumps, black	Everyday tote bag, black
431	Casual pant, taupe or mushroom		Blouse, accent color	Parka / trench coat	Round pumps, black	Small clutch, black
432	Casual pant, taupe or mushroom		Blouse, accent color	Parka / trench coat	Ballet flats, black	Everyday tote bag, black
433	Casual pant, taupe or mushroom		Blouse, accent color	Parka / trench coat	Ballet flats, black	Small clutch, black
434	Casual pant, taupe or mushroom		Blouse, accent color	Cardigan, black	Round pumps, black	Everyday tote bag, black
435	Casual pant, taupe or mushroom		Blouse, accent color	Cardigan, black	Round pumps, black	Everyday tote bag, tan

	TROUSER/ PANT	SKIRT/ SHORTS/ DRESS	TOP	OUTERWEAR	SHOE	BAG
436	Casual pant, taupe or mushroom		Blouse, accent color	Cardigan, black	Round pumps, black	Small clutch, black
437	Casual pant, taupe or mushroom		Blouse, accent color	Cardigan, black	Ballet flats, black	Everyday tote bag, black
438	Casual pant, taupe or mushroom		Blouse, accent color	Cardigan, black	Ballet flats, black	Everyday tote bag, tan
439	Casual pant, taupe or mushroom		Blouse, accent color	Cardigan, black	Ballet flats, black	Small clutch, black
440	Casual pant, taupe or mushroom		Blouse, accent color	Cardigan, black	Dressy sandals	Everyday tote bag, black
441	Casual pant, taupe or mushroom		Blouse, accent color	Cardigan, black	Dressy sandals	Everyday tote bag, tan
442	Casual pant, taupe or mushroom		Blouse, accent color	Cardigan, black	Dressy sandals	Small clutch, black
443	Casual pant, taupe or mushroom		Blouse, accent color	Cardigan, black	Wedges, tan	Everyday tote bag, tan
444	Casual pant, taupe or mushroom		Blouse, accent color	Cardigan, black	Wedges, tan	Everyday tote bag, black
445	Casual pant, taupe or mushroom		Blouse, accent color	Casual jacket	Round pumps, black	Everyday tote bag, black

	TROUSER/ PANT	SKIRT/ SHORTS/ DRESS	TOP	OUTERWEAR	SHOE	BAG
446	Casual pant, taupe or mushroom		Blouse, accent color	Casual jacket	Round pumps, black	Everyday tote bag, tan
447	Casual pant, taupe or mushroom		Blouse, accent color	Casual jacket	Round pumps, black	Small clutch, black
448	Casual pant, taupe or mushroom		Blouse, accent color	Casual jacket	Ballet flats, black	Everyday tote bag, black
449	Casual pant, taupe or mushroom		Blouse, accent color	Casual jacket	Ballet flats, black	Everyday tote bag, tan
450	Casual pant, taupe or mushroom		Blouse, accent color	Casual jacket	Ballet flats, black	Small clutch, black
451	Casual pant, taupe or mushroom		Blouse, accent color	Casual jacket	Dressy sandals	Everyday tote bag, black
452	Casual pant, taupe or mushroom		Blouse, accent color	Casual jacket	Dressy sandals	Everyday tote bag, tan
453	Casual pant, taupe or mushroom		Blouse, accent color	Casual jacket	Dressy sandals	Small clutch, black
454	Casual pant, taupe or mushroom		Blouse, accent color	Casual jacket	Wedges, tan	Everyday tote bag, tan
455	Casual pant, taupe or mushroom		Blouse, accent color	Casual jacket	Wedges, tan	Everyday tote bag, black
456	Casual pant, taupe or mushroom		Second blouse, accent color		Round pumps, black	Everyday tote bag, black

	TROUSER/ PANT	SKIRT/ SHORTS/ DRESS	TOP	OUTERWEAR	SHOE	BAG
4 5 7	Casual pant, taupe or mushroom		Second blouse, accent color		Round pumps, black	Small clutch, black
4 5 8	Casual pant, taupe or mushroom		Second blouse, accent color		Ballet flats, black	Everyday tote bag, black
4 5 9	Casual pant, taupe or mushroom		Second blouse, accent color		Ballet flats, black	Small clutch, black
4 6 0	Casual pant, taupe or mushroom		Second blouse, accent color		Dressy sandals	Everyday tote bag, tan
4 6 1	Casual pant, taupe or mushroom		Second blouse, accent color		Wedges, tan	Everyday tote bag, tan
4 6 2	Casual pant, taupe or mushroom		Second blouse, accent color	Parka / trench coat	Round pumps, black	Everyday tote bag, black
4 6 3	Casual pant, taupe or mushroom		Second blouse, accent color	Parka / trench coat	Round pumps, black	Small clutch, black
4 6 4	Casual pant, taupe or mushroom		Second blouse, accent color	Parka / trench coat	Ballet flats, black	Everyday tote bag, black
4 6 5	Casual pant, taupe or mushroom		Second blouse, accent color	Parka / trench coat	Ballet flats, black	Small clutch, black
4 6 6	Casual pant, taupe or mushroom		Second blouse, accent color	Cardigan, black	Round pumps, black	Everyday tote bag, black
4 6 7	Casual pant, taupe or mushroom		Second blouse, accent color	Cardigan, black	Round pumps, black	Everyday tote bag, tan

	TROUSER/ PANT	SKIRT/ SHORTS/ DRESS	TOP	OUTERWEAR	SHOE	BAG
468	Casual pant, taupe or mushroom		Second blouse, accent color	Cardigan, black	Round pumps, black	Small clutch, black
469	Casual pant, taupe or mushroom		Second blouse, accent color	Cardigan, black	Ballet flats, black	Everyday tote bag, black
470	Casual pant, taupe or mushroom		Second blouse, accent color	Cardigan, black	Ballet flats, black	Everyday tote bag, tan
471	Casual pant, taupe or mushroom		Second blouse, accent color	Cardigan, black	Ballet flats, black	Small clutch, black
472	Casual pant, taupe or mushroom		Second blouse, accent color	Cardigan, black	Dressy sandals	Everyday tote bag, black
473	Casual pant, taupe or mushroom		Second blouse, accent color	Cardigan, black	Dressy sandals	Everyday tote bag, tan
474	Casual pant, taupe or mushroom		Second blouse, accent color	Cardigan, black	Dressy sandals	Small clutch, black
475	Casual pant, taupe or mushroom		Second blouse, accent color	Cardigan, black	Wedges, tan	Everyday tote bag, tan
476	Casual pant, taupe or mushroom		Second blouse, accent color	Cardigan, black	Wedges, tan	Everyday tote bag, black
477	Casual pant, taupe or mushroom		Second blouse, accent color	Casual jacket	Round pumps, black	Everyday tote bag, black
478	Casual pant, taupe or mushroom		Second blouse, accent color	Casual jacket	Round pumps, black	Everyday tote bag, tan

	TROUSER/ PANT	SKIRT/ SHORTS/ DRESS	TOP	OUTERWEAR	SHOE	BAG
479	Casual pant, taupe or mushroom		Second blouse, accent color	Casual jacket	Round pumps, black	Small clutch, black
480	Casual pant, taupe or mushroom		Second blouse, accent color	Casual jacket	Ballet flats, black	Everyday tote bag, black
481	Casual pant, taupe or mushroom		Second blouse, accent color	Casual jacket	Ballet flats, black	Everyday tote bag, tan
482	Casual pant, taupe or mushroom		Second blouse, accent color	Casual jacket	Ballet flats, black	Small clutch, black
483	Casual pant, taupe or mushroom		Second blouse, accent color	Casual jacket	Dressy sandals	Everyday tote bag, black
484	Casual pant, taupe or mushroom		Second blouse, accent color	Casual jacket	Dressy sandals	Everyday tote bag, tan
485	Casual pant, taupe or mushroom		Second blouse, accent color	Casual jacket	Dressy sandals	Small clutch, black
486	Casual pant, taupe or mushroom		Second blouse, accent color	Casual jacket	Wedges, tan	Everyday tote bag, tan
487	Casual pant, taupe or mushroom		Second blouse, accent color	Casual jacket	Wedges, tan	Everyday tote bag, black
488	Casual pant, taupe or mushroom		Three-quarter sleeved top, black		Round pumps, black	Everyday tote bag, black

	TROUSER/ PANT	SKIRT/ SHORTS/ DRESS	TOP	OUTERWEAR	SHOE	BAG
489	Casual pant, taupe or mushroom		Three-quarter sleeved top, black		Round pumps, black	Small clutch, black
490	Casual pant, taupe or mushroom		Three-quarter sleeved top, black		Ballet flats, black	Everyday tote bag, black
491	Casual pant, taupe or mushroom		Three-quarter sleeved top, black		Ballet flats, black	Small clutch, black
492	Casual pant, taupe or mushroom		Three-quarter sleeved top, black		Dressy sandals	Everyday tote bag, tan
493	Casual pant, taupe or mushroom		Three-quarter sleeved top, black		Wedges, tan	Everyday tote bag, tan
494	Casual pant, taupe or mushroom		Three-quarter sleeved top, black	Parka / trench coat	Round pumps, black	Everyday tote bag, black
495	Casual pant, taupe or mushroom		Three-quarter sleeved top, black	Parka / trench coat	Round pumps, black	Small clutch, black
496	Casual pant, taupe or mushroom		Three-quarter sleeved top, black	Parka / trench coat	Ballet flats, black	Everyday tote bag, black
497	Casual pant, taupe or mushroom		Three-quarter sleeved top, black	Parka / trench coat	Ballet flats, black	Small clutch, black
498	Casual pant, taupe or mushroom		Three-quarter sleeved top, black	Cardigan, black	Round pumps, black	Everyday tote bag, black
499	Casual pant, taupe or mushroom		Three-quarter sleeved top, black	Cardigan, black	Round pumps, black	Small clutch, black

	TROUSER/ PANT	SKIRT/ SHORTS/ DRESS	TOP	OUTERWEAR	SHOE	BAG
500	Casual pant, taupe or mushroom		Three-quarter sleeved top, black	Cardigan, black	Ballet flats, black	Everyday tote bag, black
501	Casual pant, taupe or mushroom		Three-quarter sleeved top, black	Cardigan, black	Ballet flats, black	Small clutch, black
502	Casual pant, taupe or mushroom		Three-quarter sleeved top, black	Cardigan, black	Dressy sandals	Everyday tote bag, tan
503	Casual pant, taupe or mushroom		Three-quarter sleeved top, black	Cardigan, black	Wedges, tan	Everyday tote bag, tan
504	Casual pant, taupe or mushroom		Three-quarter sleeved top, black	Casual jacket	Wedges, tan	Everyday tote bag, tan
505	Casual pant, taupe or mushroom		Three-quarter sleeved top, black	Casual jacket	Ballet flats, black	Everyday tote bag, black
506	Casual pant, taupe or mushroom		Three-quarter sleeved top, black	Casual jacket	Dressy sandals	Everyday tote bag, tan
507	Casual pant, taupe or mushroom		Three-quarter sleeved top, accent color		Round pumps, black	Everyday tote bag, black
508	Casual pant, taupe or mushroom		Three-quarter sleeved top, accent color		Round pumps, black	Small clutch, black
509	Casual pant, taupe or mushroom		Three-quarter sleeved top, accent color		Ballet flats, black	Everyday tote bag, black

	TROUSER/PANT	SKIRT/SHORTS/DRESS	TOP	OUTERWEAR	SHOE	BAG
510	Casual pant, taupe or mushroom		Three-quarter sleeved top, accent color		Ballet flats, black	Small clutch, black
511	Casual pant, taupe or mushroom		Three-quarter sleeved top, accent color		Dressy sandals	Everyday tote bag, tan
512	Casual pant, taupe or mushroom		Three-quarter sleeved top, accent color		Wedges, tan	Everyday tote bag, tan
513	Casual pant, taupe or mushroom		Three-quarter sleeved top, accent color	Parka / trench coat	Round pumps, black	Everyday tote bag, black
514	Casual pant, taupe or mushroom		Three-quarter sleeved top, accent color	Parka / trench coat	Round pumps, black	Small clutch, black
515	Casual pant, taupe or mushroom		Three-quarter sleeved top, accent color	Parka / trench coat	Ballet flats, black	Everyday tote bag, black
516	Casual pant, taupe or mushroom		Three-quarter sleeved top, accent color	Parka / trench coat	Ballet flats, black	Small clutch, black
517	Casual pant, taupe or mushroom		Three-quarter sleeved top, accent color	Cardigan, black	Round pumps, black	Everyday tote bag, black
518	Casual pant, taupe or mushroom		Three-quarter sleeved top, accent color	Cardigan, black	Round pumps, black	Everyday tote bag, tan
519	Casual pant, taupe or mushroom		Three-quarter sleeved top, accent color	Cardigan, black	Round pumps, black	Small clutch, black
520	Casual pant, taupe or mushroom		Three-quarter sleeved top, accent color	Cardigan, black	Ballet flats, black	Everyday tote bag, black

	TROUSER/ PANT	SKIRT/ SHORTS/ DRESS	TOP	OUTERWEAR	SHOE	BAG
521	Casual pant, taupe or mushroom		Three-quarter sleeved top, accent color	Cardigan, black	Ballet flats, black	Everyday tote bag, tan
522	Casual pant, taupe or mushroom		Three-quarter sleeved top, accent color	Cardigan, black	Ballet flats, black	Small clutch, black
523	Casual pant, taupe or mushroom		Three-quarter sleeved top, accent color	Cardigan, black	Dressy sandals	Everyday tote bag, black
524	Casual pant, taupe or mushroom		Three-quarter sleeved top, accent color	Cardigan, black	Dressy sandals	Everyday tote bag, tan
525	Casual pant, taupe or mushroom		Three-quarter sleeved top, accent color	Cardigan, black	Dressy sandals	Small clutch, black
526	Casual pant, taupe or mushroom		Three-quarter sleeved top, accent color	Cardigan, black	Wedges, tan	Everyday tote bag, tan
527	Casual pant, taupe or mushroom		Three-quarter sleeved top, accent color	Cardigan, black	Wedges, tan	Everyday tote bag, black
528	Casual pant, taupe or mushroom		Three-quarter sleeved top, accent color	Casual jacket	Round pumps, black	Everyday tote bag, black
529	Casual pant, taupe or mushroom		Three-quarter sleeved top, accent color	Casual jacket	Round pumps, black	Everyday tote bag, tan
530	Casual pant, taupe or mushroom		Three-quarter sleeved top, accent color	Casual jacket	Round pumps, black	Small clutch, black
531	Casual pant, taupe or mushroom		Three-quarter sleeved top, accent color	Casual jacket	Ballet flats, black	Everyday tote bag, black

	TROUSER/ PANT	SKIRT/ SHORTS/ DRESS	TOP	OUTERWEAR	SHOE	BAG
532	Casual pant, taupe or mushroom		Three-quarter sleeved top, accent color	Casual jacket	Ballet flats, black	Everyday tote bag, tan
533	Casual pant, taupe or mushroom		Three-quarter sleeved top, accent color	Casual jacket	Ballet flats, black	Small clutch, black
534	Casual pant, taupe or mushroom		Three-quarter sleeved top, accent color	Casual jacket	Dressy sandals	Everyday tote bag, black
535	Casual pant, taupe or mushroom		Three-quarter sleeved top, accent color	Casual jacket	Dressy sandals	Everyday tote bag, tan
536	Casual pant, taupe or mushroom		Three-quarter sleeved top, accent color	Casual jacket	Dressy sandals	Small clutch, black
537	Casual pant, taupe or mushroom		Three-quarter sleeved top, accent color	Casual jacket	Wedges, tan	Everyday tote bag, tan
538	Casual pant, taupe or mushroom		Three-quarter sleeved top, accent color	Casual jacket	Wedges, tan	Everyday tote bag, black
539	Tailored pant, black		Basic tank, black		Round pumps, black	Everyday tote bag, black
540	Tailored pant, black		Basic tank, black		Round pumps, black	Small clutch, black
541	Tailored pant, black		Basic tank, black		Ballet flats, black	Everyday tote bag, black
542	Tailored pant, black		Basic tank, black		Strappy heel, black	Everyday tote bag, black
543	Tailored pant, black		Basic tank, black		Strappy heel, black	Small clutch, black

	TROUSER/ PANT	SKIRT/ SHORTS/ DRESS	TOP	OUTERWEAR	SHOE	BAG
544	Tailored pant, black		Basic tank, black	Parka / trench coat	Knee-high boots, black	Everyday tote bag, black
545	Tailored pant, black		Basic tank, black	Parka / trench coat	Knee-high boots, black	Small clutch, black
546	Tailored pant, black		Basic tank, black	Parka / trench coat	Round pumps, black	Everyday tote bag, black
547	Tailored pant, black		Basic tank, black	Parka / trench coat	Round pumps, black	Small clutch, black
548	Tailored pant, black		Basic tank, black	Parka / trench coat	Wedges, tan	Everyday tote bag, tan
549	Tailored pant, black		Basic tank, black	Parka / trench coat	Ballet flats, black	Everyday tote bag, black
550	Tailored pant, black		Basic tank, black	Cardigan, black	Knee-high boots, black	Everyday tote bag, black
551	Tailored pant, black		Basic tank, black	Cardigan, black	Knee-high boots, black	Small clutch, black
552	Tailored pant, black		Basic tank, black	Cardigan, black	Round pumps, black	Everyday tote bag, black
553	Tailored pant, black		Basic tank, black	Cardigan, black	Round pumps, black	Small clutch, black
554	Tailored pant, black		Basic tank, black	Cardigan, black	Wedges, tan	Everyday tote bag, tan
555	Tailored pant, black		Basic tank, black	Cardigan, black	Ballet flats, black	Everyday tote bag, black
556	Tailored pant, black		Basic tank, black	Cardigan, black	Strappy heel, black	Everyday tote bag, black
557	Tailored pant, black		Basic tank, black	Cardigan, black	Strappy heel, black	Small clutch, black
558	Tailored pant, black		Basic tank, black	Blazer, black	Knee-high boots, black	Everyday tote bag, black
559	Tailored pant, black		Basic tank, black	Blazer, black	Knee-high boots, black	Small clutch, black

	TROUSER/ PANT	SKIRT/ SHORTS/ DRESS	TOP	OUTERWEAR	SHOE	BAG
560	Tailored pant, black		Basic tank, black	Blazer, black	Round pumps, black	Everyday tote bag, black
561	Tailored pant, black		Basic tank, black	Blazer, black	Round pumps, black	Small clutch, black
562	Tailored pant, black		Basic tank, black	Blazer, black	Wedges, tan	Everyday tote bag, tan
563	Tailored pant, black		Basic tank, black	Blazer, black	Ballet flats, black	Everyday tote bag, black
564	Tailored pant, black		Basic tank, black	Blazer, black	Ballet flats, black	Small clutch, black
565	Tailored pant, black		Basic tank, black	Blazer, black	Strappy heel, black	Everyday tote bag, black
566	Tailored pant, black		Basic tank, black	Blazer, black	Strappy heel, black	Small clutch, black
567	Tailored pant, black		Basic tank, black	Blazer, stone	Knee-high boots, black	Everyday tote bag, black
568	Tailored pant, black		Basic tank, black	Blazer, stone	Knee-high boots, black	Small clutch, black
569	Tailored pant, black		Basic tank, black	Blazer, stone	Round pumps, black	Everyday tote bag, black
570	Tailored pant, black		Basic tank, black	Blazer, stone	Round pumps, black	Small clutch, black
571	Tailored pant, black		Basic tank, black	Blazer, stone	Wedges, tan	Everyday tote bag, tan
572	Tailored pant, black		Basic tank, black	Blazer, stone	Ballet flats, black	Everyday tote bag, black
573	Tailored pant, black		Basic tank, black	Blazer, stone	Strappy heel, black	Everyday tote bag, black
574	Tailored pant, black		Basic tank, black	Blazer, stone	Strappy heel, black	Small clutch, black
575	Tailored pant, black		Basic tank, black	Casual jacket	Knee-high boots, black	Everyday tote bag, black

	TROUSER/PANT	SKIRT/SHORTS/DRESS	TOP	OUTERWEAR	SHOE	BAG
576	Tailored pant, black		Basic tank, black	Casual jacket	Knee-high boots, black	Small clutch, black
577	Tailored pant, black		Basic tank, black	Casual jacket	Round pumps, black	Everyday tote bag, black
578	Tailored pant, black		Basic tank, black	Casual jacket	Round pumps, black	Small clutch, black
579	Tailored pant, black		Basic tank, black	Casual jacket	Wedges, tan	Everyday tote bag, tan
580	Tailored pant, black		Basic tank, black	Casual jacket	Ballet flats, black	Everyday tote bag, black
581	Tailored pant, black		Basic tank, white		Round pumps, black	Everyday tote bag, black
582	Tailored pant, black		Basic tank, white		Round pumps, black	Everyday tote bag, tan
583	Tailored pant, black		Basic tank, white		Round pumps, black	Small clutch, black
584	Tailored pant, black		Basic tank, white		Ballet flats, black	Everyday tote bag, black
585	Tailored pant, black		Basic tank, white		Ballet flats, black	Everyday tote bag, tan
586	Tailored pant, black		Basic tank, white		Ballet flats, black	Small clutch, black
587	Tailored pant, black		Basic tank, white		Strappy heel, black	Everyday tote bag, black
588	Tailored pant, black		Basic tank, white		Strappy heel, black	Everyday tote bag, tan
589	Tailored pant, black		Basic tank, white		Strappy heel, black	Small clutch, black
590	Tailored pant, black		Basic tank, white	Parka / trench coat	Knee-high boots, black	Everyday tote bag, black
591	Tailored pant, black		Basic tank, white	Parka / trench coat	Knee-high boots, black	Small clutch, black

	TROUSER/PANT	SKIRT/SHORTS/DRESS	TOP	OUTERWEAR	SHOE	BAG
592	Tailored pant, black		Basic tank, white	Parka / trench coat	Round pumps, black	Everyday tote bag, black
593	Tailored pant, black		Basic tank, white	Parka / trench coat	Round pumps, black	Everyday tote bag, tan
594	Tailored pant, black		Basic tank, white	Parka / trench coat	Round pumps, black	Small clutch, black
595	Tailored pant, black		Basic tank, white	Parka / trench coat	Wedges, tan	Everyday tote bag, tan
596	Tailored pant, black		Basic tank, white	Parka / trench coat	Ballet flats, black	Everyday tote bag, black
597	Tailored pant, black		Basic tank, white	Parka / trench coat	Ballet flats, black	Everyday tote bag, tan
598	Tailored pant, black		Basic tank, white	Cardigan, black	Knee-high boots, black	Everyday tote bag, black
599	Tailored pant, black		Basic tank, white	Cardigan, black	Knee-high boots, black	Everyday tote bag, tan
600	Tailored pant, black		Basic tank, white	Cardigan, black	Knee-high boots, black	Small clutch, black
601	Tailored pant, black		Basic tank, white	Cardigan, black	Round pumps, black	Everyday tote bag, black
602	Tailored pant, black		Basic tank, white	Cardigan, black	Round pumps, black	Everyday tote bag, tan
603	Tailored pant, black		Basic tank, white	Cardigan, black	Round pumps, black	Small clutch, black
604	Tailored pant, black		Basic tank, white	Cardigan, black	Wedges, tan	Everyday tote bag, tan
605	Tailored pant, black		Basic tank, white	Cardigan, black	Ballet flats, black	Everyday tote bag, black
606	Tailored pant, black		Basic tank, white	Cardigan, black	Ballet flats, black	Everyday tote bag, tan
607	Tailored pant, black		Basic tank, white	Cardigan, black	Strappy heel, black	Everyday tote bag, black

	TROUSER/PANT	SKIRT/SHORTS/DRESS	TOP	OUTERWEAR	SHOE	BAG
608	Tailored pant, black		Basic tank, white	Cardigan, black	Strappy heel, black	Everyday tote bag, tan
609	Tailored pant, black		Basic tank, white	Cardigan, black	Strappy heel, black	Small clutch, black
610	Tailored pant, black		Basic tank, white	Blazer, black	Knee-high boots, black	Everyday tote bag, black
611	Tailored pant, black		Basic tank, white	Blazer, black	Knee-high boots, black	Everyday tote bag, tan
612	Tailored pant, black		Basic tank, white	Blazer, black	Knee-high boots, black	Small clutch, black
613	Tailored pant, black		Basic tank, white	Blazer, black	Round pumps, black	Everyday tote bag, black
614	Tailored pant, black		Basic tank, white	Blazer, black	Round pumps, black	Everyday tote bag, tan
615	Tailored pant, black		Basic tank, white	Blazer, black	Round pumps, black	Small clutch, black
616	Tailored pant, black		Basic tank, white	Blazer, black	Wedges, tan	Everyday tote bag, tan
617	Tailored pant, black		Basic tank, white	Blazer, black	Ballet flats, black	Everyday tote bag, black
618	Tailored pant, black		Basic tank, white	Blazer, black	Ballet flats, black	Everyday tote bag, tan
619	Tailored pant, black		Basic tank, white	Blazer, black	Ballet flats, black	Small clutch, black
620	Tailored pant, black		Basic tank, white	Blazer, black	Strappy heel, black	Everyday tote bag, black
621	Tailored pant, black		Basic tank, white	Blazer, black	Strappy heel, black	Everyday tote bag, tan
622	Tailored pant, black		Basic tank, white	Blazer, black	Strappy heel, black	Small clutch, black
623	Tailored pant, black		Basic tank, white	Blazer, stone	Knee-high boots, black	Everyday tote bag, black

	TROUSER/ PANT	SKIRT/ SHORTS/ DRESS	TOP	OUTERWEAR	SHOE	BAG
624	Tailored pant, black		Basic tank, white	Blazer, stone	Knee-high boots, black	Everyday tote bag, tan
625	Tailored pant, black		Basic tank, white	Blazer, stone	Knee-high boots, black	Small clutch, black
626	Tailored pant, black		Basic tank, white	Blazer, stone	Round pumps, black	Everyday tote bag, black
627	Tailored pant, black		Basic tank, white	Blazer, stone	Round pumps, black	Everyday tote bag, tan
628	Tailored pant, black		Basic tank, white	Blazer, stone	Round pumps, black	Small clutch, black
629	Tailored pant, black		Basic tank, white	Blazer, stone	Wedges, tan	Everyday tote bag, tan
630	Tailored pant, black		Basic tank, white	Blazer, stone	Ballet flats, black	Everyday tote bag, black
631	Tailored pant, black		Basic tank, white	Blazer, stone	Ballet flats, black	Everyday tote bag, tan
632	Tailored pant, black		Basic tank, white	Blazer, stone	Ballet flats, black	Small clutch, black
633	Tailored pant, black		Basic tank, white	Blazer, stone	Strappy heel, black	Everyday tote bag, black
634	Tailored pant, black		Basic tank, white	Blazer, stone	Strappy heel, black	Everyday tote bag, tan
635	Tailored pant, black		Basic tank, white	Blazer, stone	Strappy heel, black	Small clutch, black
636	Tailored pant, black		Basic tank, white	Casual jacket	Knee-high boots, black	Everyday tote bag, black
637	Tailored pant, black		Basic tank, white	Casual jacket	Knee-high boots, black	Everyday tote bag, tan
638	Tailored pant, black		Basic tank, white	Casual jacket	Round pumps, black	Everyday tote bag, black
639	Tailored pant, black		Basic tank, white	Casual jacket	Round pumps, black	Everyday tote bag, tan

	TROUSER/PANT	SKIRT/SHORTS/DRESS	TOP	OUTERWEAR	SHOE	BAG
640	Tailored pant, black		Basic tank, white	Casual jacket	Round pumps, black	Small clutch, black
641	Tailored pant, black		Basic tank, white	Casual jacket	Wedges, tan	Everyday tote bag, tan
642	Tailored pant, black		Basic tank, white	Casual jacket	Ballet flats, black	Everyday tote bag, black
643	Tailored pant, black		Basic tank, white	Casual jacket	Ballet flats, black	Everyday tote bag, tan
644	Tailored pant, black		Basic tank, white	Casual jacket	Strappy heel, black	Everyday tote bag, black
645	Tailored pant, black		Basic tank, white	Casual jacket	Strappy heel, black	Everyday tote bag, tan
646	Tailored pant, black		Blouse, accent color		Round pumps, black	Everyday tote bag, black
647	Tailored pant, black		Blouse, accent color		Round pumps, black	Small clutch, black
648	Tailored pant, black		Blouse, accent color		Ballet flats, black	Everyday tote bag, black
649	Tailored pant, black		Blouse, accent color		Strappy heel, black	Everyday tote bag, black
650	Tailored pant, black		Blouse, accent color		Strappy heel, black	Small clutch, black
651	Tailored pant, black		Blouse, accent color	Parka / trench coat	Knee-high boots, black	Everyday tote bag, black
652	Tailored pant, black		Blouse, accent color	Parka / trench coat	Knee-high boots, black	Small clutch, black
653	Tailored pant, black		Blouse, accent color	Parka / trench coat	Round pumps, black	Everyday tote bag, black
654	Tailored pant, black		Blouse, accent color	Parka / trench coat	Round pumps, black	Small clutch, black
655	Tailored pant, black		Blouse, accent color	Parka / trench coat	Wedges, tan	Everyday tote bag, tan

	TROUSER/ PANT	SKIRT/ SHORTS/ DRESS	TOP	OUTERWEAR	SHOE	BAG
656	Tailored pant, black		Blouse, accent color	Parka / trench coat	Ballet flats, black	Everyday tote bag, black
657	Tailored pant, black		Blouse, accent color	Parka / trench coat	Ballet flats, black	Small clutch, black
658	Tailored pant, black		Blouse, accent color	Cardigan, black	Knee-high boots, black	Everyday tote bag, black
659	Tailored pant, black		Blouse, accent color	Cardigan, black	Knee-high boots, black	Small clutch, black
660	Tailored pant, black		Blouse, accent color	Cardigan, black	Round pumps, black	Everyday tote bag, black
661	Tailored pant, black		Blouse, accent color	Cardigan, black	Round pumps, black	Small clutch, black
662	Tailored pant, black		Blouse, accent color	Cardigan, black	Wedges, tan	Everyday tote bag, tan
663	Tailored pant, black		Blouse, accent color	Cardigan, black	Ballet flats, black	Everyday tote bag, black
664	Tailored pant, black		Blouse, accent color	Cardigan, black	Ballet flats, black	Small clutch, black
665	Tailored pant, black		Blouse, accent color	Cardigan, black	Strappy heel, black	Everyday tote bag, black
666	Tailored pant, black		Blouse, accent color	Cardigan, black	Strappy heel, black	Small clutch, black
667	Tailored pant, black		Blouse, accent color	Blazer, black	Knee-high boots, black	Everyday tote bag, black
668	Tailored pant, black		Blouse, accent color	Blazer, black	Knee-high boots, black	Small clutch, black
669	Tailored pant, black		Blouse, accent color	Blazer, black	Round pumps, black	Everyday tote bag, black
670	Tailored pant, black		Blouse, accent color	Blazer, black	Round pumps, black	Small clutch, black
671	Tailored pant, black		Blouse, accent color	Blazer, black	Wedges, tan	Everyday tote bag, tan

	TROUSER/ PANT	SKIRT/ SHORTS/ DRESS	TOP	OUTERWEAR	SHOE	BAG
672	Tailored pant, black		Blouse, accent color	Blazer, black	Ballet flats, black	Everyday tote bag, black
673	Tailored pant, black		Blouse, accent color	Blazer, black	Ballet flats, black	Small clutch, black
674	Tailored pant, black		Blouse, accent color	Blazer, black	Strappy heel, black	Everyday tote bag, black
675	Tailored pant, black		Blouse, accent color	Blazer, black	Strappy heel, black	Small clutch, black
676	Tailored pant, black		Blouse, accent color	Blazer, stone	Knee-high boots, black	Everyday tote bag, black
677	Tailored pant, black		Blouse, accent color	Blazer, stone	Knee-high boots, black	Everyday tote bag, tan
678	Tailored pant, black		Blouse, accent color	Blazer, stone	Knee-high boots, black	Small clutch, black
679	Tailored pant, black		Blouse, accent color	Blazer, stone	Round pumps, black	Everyday tote bag, black
680	Tailored pant, black		Blouse, accent color	Blazer, stone	Round pumps, black	Everyday tote bag, tan
681	Tailored pant, black		Blouse, accent color	Blazer, stone	Round pumps, black	Small clutch, black
682	Tailored pant, black		Blouse, accent color	Blazer, stone	Wedges, tan	Everyday tote bag, tan
683	Tailored pant, black		Blouse, accent color	Blazer, stone	Ballet flats, black	Everyday tote bag, black
684	Tailored pant, black		Blouse, accent color	Blazer, stone	Ballet flats, black	Everyday tote bag, tan
685	Tailored pant, black		Blouse, accent color	Blazer, stone	Ballet flats, black	Small clutch, black
686	Tailored pant, black		Blouse, accent color	Blazer, stone	Strappy heel, black	Everyday tote bag, black

	TROUSER/ PANT	SKIRT/ SHORTS/ DRESS	TOP	OUTERWEAR	SHOE	BAG
687	Tailored pant, black		Blouse, accent color	Blazer, stone	Strappy heel, black	Everyday tote bag, tan
688	Tailored pant, black		Blouse, accent color	Blazer, stone	Strappy heel, black	Small clutch, black
689	Tailored pant, black		Blouse, accent color	Casual jacket	Knee-high boots, black	Everyday tote bag, black
690	Tailored pant, black		Blouse, accent color	Casual jacket	Knee-high boots, black	Everyday tote bag, tan
691	Tailored pant, black		Blouse, accent color	Casual jacket	Knee-high boots, black	Small clutch, black
692	Tailored pant, black		Blouse, accent color	Casual jacket	Round pumps, black	Everyday tote bag, black
693	Tailored pant, black		Blouse, accent color	Casual jacket	Round pumps, black	Everyday tote bag, tan
694	Tailored pant, black		Blouse, accent color	Casual jacket	Round pumps, black	Small clutch, black
695	Tailored pant, black		Blouse, accent color	Casual jacket	Wedges, tan	Everyday tote bag, tan
696	Tailored pant, black		Blouse, accent color	Casual jacket	Ballet flats, black	Everyday tote bag, black
697	Tailored pant, black		Blouse, accent color	Casual jacket	Ballet flats, black	Everyday tote bag, tan
698	Tailored pant, black		Blouse, accent color	Casual jacket	Strappy heel, black	Everyday tote bag, black
699	Tailored pant, black		Blouse, accent color	Casual jacket	Strappy heel, black	Everyday tote bag, tan
700	Tailored pant, black		Blouse, accent color	Casual jacket	Strappy heel, black	Small clutch, black
701	Tailored pant, black		Second blouse, accent color		Round pumps, black	Everyday tote bag, black
702	Tailored pant, black		Second blouse, accent color		Round pumps, black	Small clutch, black

	TROUSER/ PANT	SKIRT/ SHORTS/ DRESS	TOP	OUTERWEAR	SHOE	BAG
703	Tailored pant, black		Second blouse, accent color		Ballet flats, black	Everyday tote bag, black
704	Tailored pant, black		Second blouse, accent color		Strappy heel, black	Everyday tote bag, black
705	Tailored pant, black		Second blouse, accent color		Strappy heel, black	Small clutch, black
706	Tailored pant, black		Second blouse, accent color	Parka / trench coat	Knee-high boots, black	Everyday tote bag, black
707	Tailored pant, black		Second blouse, accent color	Parka / trench coat	Knee-high boots, black	Small clutch, black
708	Tailored pant, black		Second blouse, accent color	Parka / trench coat	Round pumps, black	Everyday tote bag, black
709	Tailored pant, black		Second blouse, accent color	Parka / trench coat	Round pumps, black	Small clutch, black
710	Tailored pant, black		Second blouse, accent color	Parka / trench coat	Wedges, tan	Everyday tote bag, tan
711	Tailored pant, black		Second blouse, accent color	Parka / trench coat	Ballet flats, black	Everyday tote bag, black
712	Tailored pant, black		Second blouse, accent color	Parka / trench coat	Ballet flats, black	Small clutch, black
713	Tailored pant, black		Second blouse, accent color	Cardigan, black	Knee-high boots, black	Everyday tote bag, black
714	Tailored pant, black		Second blouse, accent color	Cardigan, black	Knee-high boots, black	Small clutch, black
715	Tailored pant, black		Second blouse, accent color	Cardigan, black	Round pumps, black	Everyday tote bag, black
716	Tailored pant, black		Second blouse, accent color	Cardigan, black	Round pumps, black	Small clutch, black
717	Tailored pant, black		Second blouse, accent color	Cardigan, black	Wedges, tan	Everyday tote bag, tan

	TROUSER/PANT	SKIRT/SHORTS/DRESS	TOP	OUTERWEAR	SHOE	BAG
718	Tailored pant, black		Second blouse, accent color	Cardigan, black	Ballet flats, black	Everyday tote bag, black
719	Tailored pant, black		Second blouse, accent color	Cardigan, black	Ballet flats, black	Small clutch, black
720	Tailored pant, black		Second blouse, accent color	Cardigan, black	Strappy heel, black	Everyday tote bag, black
721	Tailored pant, black		Second blouse, accent color	Cardigan, black	Strappy heel, black	Small clutch, black
722	Tailored pant, black		Second blouse, accent color	Blazer, black	Knee-high boots, black	Everyday tote bag, black
723	Tailored pant, black		Second blouse, accent color	Blazer, black	Knee-high boots, black	Small clutch, black
724	Tailored pant, black		Second blouse, accent color	Blazer, black	Round pumps, black	Everyday tote bag, black
725	Tailored pant, black		Second blouse, accent color	Blazer, black	Round pumps, black	Small clutch, black
726	Tailored pant, black		Second blouse, accent color	Blazer, black	Wedges, tan	Everyday tote bag, tan
727	Tailored pant, black		Second blouse, accent color	Blazer, black	Ballet flats, black	Everyday tote bag, black
728	Tailored pant, black		Second blouse, accent color	Blazer, black	Ballet flats, black	Small clutch, black
729	Tailored pant, black		Second blouse, accent color	Blazer, black	Strappy heel, black	Everyday tote bag, black
730	Tailored pant, black		Second blouse, accent color	Blazer, black	Strappy heel, black	Small clutch, black
731	Tailored pant, black		Second blouse, accent color	Blazer, stone	Knee-high boots, black	Everyday tote bag, black
732	Tailored pant, black		Second blouse, accent color	Blazer, stone	Knee-high boots, black	Everyday tote bag, tan
733	Tailored pant, black		Second blouse, accent color	Blazer, stone	Knee-high boots, black	Small clutch, black

	TROUSER/ PANT	SKIRT/ SHORTS/ DRESS	TOP	OUTERWEAR	SHOE	BAG
734	Tailored pant, black		Second blouse, accent color	Blazer, stone	Round pumps, black	Everyday tote bag, black
735	Tailored pant, black		Second blouse, accent color	Blazer, stone	Round pumps, black	Everyday tote bag, tan
736	Tailored pant, black		Second blouse, accent color	Blazer, stone	Round pumps, black	Small clutch, black
737	Tailored pant, black		Second blouse, accent color	Blazer, stone	Wedges, tan	Everyday tote bag, tan
738	Tailored pant, black		Second blouse, accent color	Blazer, stone	Ballet flats, black	Everyday tote bag, black
739	Tailored pant, black		Second blouse, accent color	Blazer, stone	Ballet flats, black	Everyday tote bag, tan
740	Tailored pant, black		Second blouse, accent color	Blazer, stone	Ballet flats, black	Small clutch, black
741	Tailored pant, black		Second blouse, accent color	Blazer, stone	Strappy heel, black	Everyday tote bag, black
742	Tailored pant, black		Second blouse, accent color	Blazer, stone	Strappy heel, black	Everyday tote bag, tan
743	Tailored pant, black		Second blouse, accent color	Blazer, stone	Strappy heel, black	Small clutch, black
744	Tailored pant, black		Second blouse, accent color	Casual jacket	Knee-high boots, black	Everyday tote bag, black
745	Tailored pant, black		Second blouse, accent color	Casual jacket	Knee-high boots, black	Small clutch, black
746	Tailored pant, black		Second blouse, accent color	Casual jacket	Round pumps, black	Everyday tote bag, black
747	Tailored pant, black		Second blouse, accent color	Casual jacket	Round pumps, black	Small clutch, black
748	Tailored pant, black		Second blouse, accent color	Casual jacket	Wedges, tan	Everyday tote bag, tan
749	Tailored pant, black		Second blouse, accent color	Casual jacket	Ballet flats, black	Everyday tote bag, black

	TROUSER/ PANT	SKIRT/ SHORTS/ DRESS	TOP	OUTERWEAR	SHOE	BAG
750	Tailored pant, black		Second blouse, accent color	Casual jacket	Strappy heel, black	Everyday tote bag, black
751	Tailored pant, black		Second blouse, accent color	Casual jacket	Strappy heel, black	Small clutch, black
752	Tailored pant, black		Three-quarter sleeved top, accent color		Round pumps, black	Everyday tote bag, black
753	Tailored pant, black		Three-quarter sleeved top, accent color		Round pumps, black	Small clutch, black
754	Tailored pant, black		Three-quarter sleeved top, accent color		Ballet flats, black	Everyday tote bag, black
755	Tailored pant, black		Three-quarter sleeved top, accent color		Ballet flats, black	Small clutch, black
756	Tailored pant, black		Three-quarter sleeved top, accent color		Strappy heel, black	Everyday tote bag, black
757	Tailored pant, black		Three-quarter sleeved top, accent color		Strappy heel, black	Small clutch, black
758	Tailored pant, black		Three-quarter sleeved top, accent color	Parka / trench coat	Knee-high boots, black	Everyday tote bag, black
759	Tailored pant, black		Three-quarter sleeved top, accent color	Parka / trench coat	Round pumps, black	Everyday tote bag, black
760	Tailored pant, black		Three-quarter sleeved top, accent color	Parka / trench coat	Round pumps, black	Small clutch, black
761	Tailored pant, black		Three-quarter sleeved top, accent color	Parka / trench coat	Wedges, tan	Everyday tote bag, tan
762	Tailored pant, black		Three-quarter sleeved top, accent color	Parka / trench coat	Ballet flats, black	Everyday tote bag, black
763	Tailored pant, black		Three-quarter sleeved top, accent color	Parka / trench coat	Ballet flats, black	Small clutch, black
764	Tailored pant, black		Three-quarter sleeved top, accent color	Blazer, black	Knee-high boots, black	Everyday tote bag, black
765	Tailored pant, black		Three-quarter sleeved top, accent color	Blazer, black	Knee-high boots, black	Small clutch, black

	TROUSER/PANT	SKIRT/SHORTS/DRESS	TOP	OUTERWEAR	SHOE	BAG
766	Tailored pant, black		Three-quarter sleeved top, accent color	Blazer, black	Round pumps, black	Everyday tote bag, black
767	Tailored pant, black		Three-quarter sleeved top, accent color	Blazer, black	Round pumps, black	Small clutch, black
768	Tailored pant, black		Three-quarter sleeved top, accent color	Blazer, black	Wedges, tan	Everyday tote bag, tan
769	Tailored pant, black		Three-quarter sleeved top, accent color	Blazer, black	Ballet flats, black	Everyday tote bag, black
770	Tailored pant, black		Three-quarter sleeved top, accent color	Blazer, black	Ballet flats, black	Small clutch, black
771	Tailored pant, black		Three-quarter sleeved top, accent color	Blazer, black	Strappy heel, black	Everyday tote bag, black
772	Tailored pant, black		Three-quarter sleeved top, accent color	Blazer, black	Strappy heel, black	Small clutch, black
773	Tailored pant, black		Three-quarter sleeved top, accent color	Blazer, stone	Knee-high boots, black	Everyday tote bag, black
774	Tailored pant, black		Three-quarter sleeved top, accent color	Blazer, stone	Knee-high boots, black	Everyday tote bag, tan
775	Tailored pant, black		Three-quarter sleeved top, accent color	Blazer, stone	Knee-high boots, black	Small clutch, black
776	Tailored pant, black		Three-quarter sleeved top, accent color	Blazer, stone	Round pumps, black	Everyday tote bag, black
777	Tailored pant, black		Three-quarter sleeved top, accent color	Blazer, stone	Round pumps, black	Everyday tote bag, tan
778	Tailored pant, black		Three-quarter sleeved top, accent color	Blazer, stone	Round pumps, black	Small clutch, black
779	Tailored pant, black		Three-quarter sleeved top, accent color	Blazer, stone	Wedges, tan	Everyday tote bag, tan
780	Tailored pant, black		Three-quarter sleeved top, accent color	Blazer, stone	Ballet flats, black	Everyday tote bag, black
781	Tailored pant, black		Three-quarter sleeved top, accent color	Blazer, stone	Ballet flats, black	Everyday tote bag, tan

	TROUSER/PANT	SKIRT/SHORTS/DRESS	TOP	OUTERWEAR	SHOE	BAG
782	Tailored pant, black		Three-quarter sleeved top, accent color	Blazer, stone	Ballet flats, black	Small clutch, black
783	Tailored pant, black		Three-quarter sleeved top, accent color	Blazer, stone	Strappy heel, black	Everyday tote bag, black
784	Tailored pant, black		Three-quarter sleeved top, accent color	Blazer, stone	Strappy heel, black	Everyday tote bag, tan
785	Tailored pant, black		Three-quarter sleeved top, accent color	Blazer, stone	Strappy heel, black	Small clutch, black
786	Tailored pant, black		Three-quarter sleeved top, accent color	Casual jacket	Knee-high boots, black	Everyday tote bag, black
787	Tailored pant, black		Three-quarter sleeved top, accent color	Casual jacket	Round pumps, black	Everyday tote bag, black
788	Tailored pant, black		Three-quarter sleeved top, accent color	Casual jacket	Round pumps, black	Small clutch, black
789	Tailored pant, black		Three-quarter sleeved top, accent color	Casual jacket	Wedges, tan	Everyday tote bag, tan
790	Tailored pant, black		Three-quarter sleeved top, accent color	Casual jacket	Ballet flats, black	Everyday tote bag, black
791	Tailored pant, black		Three-quarter sleeved top, accent color	Casual jacket	Strappy heel, black	Everyday tote bag, black
792	Tailored pant, black		Three-quarter sleeved top, accent color	Casual jacket	Strappy heel, black	Small clutch, black
793	Tailored pant, black		Three-quarter sleeved top, black		Round pumps, black	Everyday tote bag, black
794	Tailored pant, black		Three-quarter sleeved top, black		Round pumps, black	Small clutch, black
795	Tailored pant, black		Three-quarter sleeved top, black		Ballet flats, black	Everyday tote bag, black
796	Tailored pant, black		Three-quarter sleeved top, black		Strappy heel, black	Everyday tote bag, black
797	Tailored pant, black		Three-quarter sleeved top, black		Strappy heel, black	Small clutch, black

	TROUSER/ PANT	SKIRT/ SHORTS/ DRESS	TOP	OUTERWEAR	SHOE	BAG
798	Tailored pant, black		Three-quarter sleeved top, black	Parka / trench coat	Knee-high boots, black	Everyday tote bag, black
799	Tailored pant, black		Three-quarter sleeved top, black	Parka / trench coat	Round pumps, black	Everyday tote bag, black
800	Tailored pant, black		Three-quarter sleeved top, black	Parka / trench coat	Round pumps, black	Small clutch, black
801	Tailored pant, black		Three-quarter sleeved top, black	Parka / trench coat	Wedges, tan	Everyday tote bag, tan
802	Tailored pant, black		Three-quarter sleeved top, black	Parka / trench coat	Ballet flats, black	Everyday tote bag, black
803	Tailored pant, black		Three-quarter sleeved top, black	Parka / trench coat	Ballet flats, black	Small clutch, black
804	Tailored pant, black		Three-quarter sleeved top, black	Blazer, black	Knee-high boots, black	Everyday tote bag, black
805	Tailored pant, black		Three-quarter sleeved top, black	Blazer, black	Knee-high boots, black	Small clutch, black
806	Tailored pant, black		Three-quarter sleeved top, black	Blazer, black	Round pumps, black	Everyday tote bag, black
807	Tailored pant, black		Three-quarter sleeved top, black	Blazer, black	Round pumps, black	Small clutch, black
808	Tailored pant, black		Three-quarter sleeved top, black	Blazer, black	Wedges, tan	Everyday tote bag, tan
809	Tailored pant, black		Three-quarter sleeved top, black	Blazer, black	Ballet flats, black	Everyday tote bag, black
810	Tailored pant, black		Three-quarter sleeved top, black	Blazer, black	Ballet flats, black	Small clutch, black
811	Tailored pant, black		Three-quarter sleeved top, black	Blazer, black	Strappy heel, black	Everyday tote bag, black
812	Tailored pant, black		Three-quarter sleeved top, black	Blazer, black	Strappy heel, black	Small clutch, black
813	Tailored pant, black		Three-quarter sleeved top, black	Blazer, stone	Knee-high boots, black	Everyday tote bag, black

	TROUSER/PANT	SKIRT/SHORTS/DRESS	TOP	OUTERWEAR	SHOE	BAG
814	Tailored pant, black		Three-quarter sleeved top, black	Blazer, stone	Knee-high boots, black	Everyday tote bag, tan
815	Tailored pant, black		Three-quarter sleeved top, black	Blazer, stone	Knee-high boots, black	Small clutch, black
816	Tailored pant, black		Three-quarter sleeved top, black	Blazer, stone	Round pumps, black	Everyday tote bag, black
817	Tailored pant, black		Three-quarter sleeved top, black	Blazer, stone	Round pumps, black	Everyday tote bag, tan
818	Tailored pant, black		Three-quarter sleeved top, black	Blazer, stone	Round pumps, black	Small clutch, black
819	Tailored pant, black		Three-quarter sleeved top, black	Blazer, stone	Wedges, tan	Everyday tote bag, tan
820	Tailored pant, black		Three-quarter sleeved top, black	Blazer, stone	Ballet flats, black	Everyday tote bag, black
821	Tailored pant, black		Three-quarter sleeved top, black	Blazer, stone	Ballet flats, black	Everyday tote bag, tan
822	Tailored pant, black		Three-quarter sleeved top, black	Blazer, stone	Ballet flats, black	Small clutch, black
823	Tailored pant, black		Three-quarter sleeved top, black	Blazer, stone	Strappy heel, black	Everyday tote bag, black
824	Tailored pant, black		Three-quarter sleeved top, black	Blazer, stone	Strappy heel, black	Everyday tote bag, tan
825	Tailored pant, black		Three-quarter sleeved top, black	Blazer, stone	Strappy heel, black	Small clutch, black
826	Tailored pant, black		Three-quarter sleeved top, black	Casual jacket	Knee-high boots, black	Everyday tote bag, black
827	Tailored pant, black		Three-quarter sleeved top, black	Casual jacket	Knee-high boots, black	Small clutch, black
828	Tailored pant, black		Three-quarter sleeved top, black	Casual jacket	Round pumps, black	Everyday tote bag, black
829	Tailored pant, black		Three-quarter sleeved top, black	Casual jacket	Round pumps, black	Small clutch, black

	TROUSER/PANT	SKIRT/SHORTS/DRESS	TOP	OUTERWEAR	SHOE	BAG
830	Tailored pant, black		Three-quarter sleeved top, black	Casual jacket	Wedges, tan	Everyday tote bag, tan
831	Tailored pant, black		Three-quarter sleeved top, black	Casual jacket	Ballet flats, black	Everyday tote bag, black
832	Tailored pant, black		Three-quarter sleeved top, black	Casual jacket	Strappy heel, black	Everyday tote bag, black
833	Tailored pant, black		Three-quarter sleeved top, black	Casual jacket	Strappy heel, black	Small clutch, black
834	Tailored pant, stone or taupe		Basic tank, black		Round pumps, black	Everyday tote bag, black
835	Tailored pant, stone or taupe		Basic tank, black		Round pumps, black	Small clutch, black
836	Tailored pant, stone or taupe		Basic tank, black		Wedges, tan	Everyday tote bag, tan
837	Tailored pant, stone or taupe		Basic tank, black		Ballet flats, black	Everyday tote bag, black
838	Tailored pant, stone or taupe		Basic tank, black		Strappy heel, black	Everyday tote bag, black
839	Tailored pant, stone or taupe		Basic tank, black		Strappy heel, black	Small clutch, black
840	Tailored pant, stone or taupe		Basic tank, black	Parka / trench coat	Knee-high boots, black	Everyday tote bag, black
841	Tailored pant, stone or taupe		Basic tank, black	Parka / trench coat	Knee-high boots, black	Small clutch, black
842	Tailored pant, stone or taupe		Basic tank, black	Parka / trench coat	Round pumps, black	Everyday tote bag, black
843	Tailored pant, stone or taupe		Basic tank, black	Parka / trench coat	Round pumps, black	Small clutch, black
844	Tailored pant, stone or taupe		Basic tank, black	Parka / trench coat	Wedges, tan	Everyday tote bag, tan
845	Tailored pant, stone or taupe		Basic tank, black	Parka / trench coat	Ballet flats, black	Everyday tote bag, black

	TROUSER/ PANT	SKIRT/ SHORTS/ DRESS	TOP	OUTERWEAR	SHOE	BAG
846	Tailored pant, stone or taupe		Basic tank, black	Parka / trench coat	Ballet flats, black	Small clutch, black
847	Tailored pant, stone or taupe		Basic tank, black	Cardigan, black	Knee-high boots, black	Everyday tote bag, black
848	Tailored pant, stone or taupe		Basic tank, black	Cardigan, black	Knee-high boots, black	Everyday tote bag, tan
849	Tailored pant, stone or taupe		Basic tank, black	Cardigan, black	Knee-high boots, black	Small clutch, black
850	Tailored pant, stone or taupe		Basic tank, black	Cardigan, black	Round pumps, black	Everyday tote bag, black
851	Tailored pant, stone or taupe		Basic tank, black	Cardigan, black	Round pumps, black	Everyday tote bag, tan
852	Tailored pant, stone or taupe		Basic tank, black	Cardigan, black	Round pumps, black	Small clutch, black
853	Tailored pant, stone or taupe		Basic tank, black	Cardigan, black	Wedges, tan	Everyday tote bag, tan
854	Tailored pant, stone or taupe		Basic tank, black	Cardigan, black	Ballet flats, black	Everyday tote bag, black
855	Tailored pant, stone or taupe		Basic tank, black	Cardigan, black	Ballet flats, black	Everyday tote bag, tan
856	Tailored pant, stone or taupe		Basic tank, black	Cardigan, black	Strappy heel, black	Everyday tote bag, black
857	Tailored pant, stone or taupe		Basic tank, black	Cardigan, black	Strappy heel, black	Everyday tote bag, tan
858	Tailored pant, stone or taupe		Basic tank, black	Cardigan, black	Strappy heel, black	Small clutch, black
859	Tailored pant, stone or taupe		Basic tank, black	Cardigan, black	Dressy sandals	Everyday tote bag, tan
860	Tailored pant, stone or taupe		Basic tank, black	Blazer, black	Knee-high boots, black	Everyday tote bag, black
861	Tailored pant, stone or taupe		Basic tank, black	Blazer, black	Knee-high boots, black	Everyday tote bag, tan

	TROUSER/PANT	SKIRT/SHORTS/DRESS	TOP	OUTERWEAR	SHOE	BAG
862	Tailored pant, stone or taupe		Basic tank, black	Blazer, black	Knee-high boots, black	Small clutch, black
863	Tailored pant, stone or taupe		Basic tank, black	Blazer, black	Round pumps, black	Everyday tote bag, black
864	Tailored pant, stone or taupe		Basic tank, black	Blazer, black	Round pumps, black	Everyday tote bag, tan
865	Tailored pant, stone or taupe		Basic tank, black	Blazer, black	Round pumps, black	Small clutch, black
866	Tailored pant, stone or taupe		Basic tank, black	Blazer, black	Wedges, tan	Everyday tote bag, tan
867	Tailored pant, stone or taupe		Basic tank, black	Blazer, black	Ballet flats, black	Everyday tote bag, black
868	Tailored pant, stone or taupe		Basic tank, black	Blazer, black	Ballet flats, black	Everyday tote bag, tan
869	Tailored pant, stone or taupe		Basic tank, black	Blazer, black	Strappy heel, black	Everyday tote bag, black
870	Tailored pant, stone or taupe		Basic tank, black	Blazer, black	Strappy heel, black	Everyday tote bag, tan
871	Tailored pant, stone or taupe		Basic tank, black	Blazer, black	Strappy heel, black	Small clutch, black
872	Tailored pant, stone or taupe		Basic tank, black	Blazer, stone	Knee-high boots, black	Everyday tote bag, black
873	Tailored pant, stone or taupe		Basic tank, black	Blazer, stone	Knee-high boots, black	Everyday tote bag, tan
874	Tailored pant, stone or taupe		Basic tank, black	Blazer, stone	Knee-high boots, black	Small clutch, black
875	Tailored pant, stone or taupe		Basic tank, black	Blazer, stone	Round pumps, black	Everyday tote bag, black
876	Tailored pant, stone or taupe		Basic tank, black	Blazer, stone	Round pumps, black	Everyday tote bag, tan
877	Tailored pant, stone or taupe		Basic tank, black	Blazer, stone	Round pumps, black	Small clutch, black

	TROUSER/ PANT	SKIRT/ SHORTS/ DRESS	TOP	OUTERWEAR	SHOE	BAG
878	Tailored pant, stone or taupe		Basic tank, black	Blazer, stone	Wedges, tan	Everyday tote bag, tan
879	Tailored pant, stone or taupe		Basic tank, black	Blazer, stone	Ballet flats, black	Everyday tote bag, black
880	Tailored pant, stone or taupe		Basic tank, black	Blazer, stone	Ballet flats, black	Everyday tote bag, tan
881	Tailored pant, stone or taupe		Basic tank, black	Blazer, stone	Strappy heel, black	Everyday tote bag, black
882	Tailored pant, stone or taupe		Basic tank, black	Blazer, stone	Strappy heel, black	Everyday tote bag, tan
883	Tailored pant, stone or taupe		Basic tank, black	Blazer, stone	Strappy heel, black	Small clutch, black
884	Tailored pant, stone or taupe		Basic tank, black	Casual jacket	Knee-high boots, black	Everyday tote bag, black
885	Tailored pant, stone or taupe		Basic tank, black	Casual jacket	Knee-high boots, black	Everyday tote bag, tan
886	Tailored pant, stone or taupe		Basic tank, black	Casual jacket	Knee-high boots, black	Small clutch, black
887	Tailored pant, stone or taupe		Basic tank, black	Casual jacket	Round pumps, black	Everyday tote bag, black
888	Tailored pant, stone or taupe		Basic tank, black	Casual jacket	Round pumps, black	Everyday tote bag, tan
889	Tailored pant, stone or taupe		Basic tank, black	Casual jacket	Round pumps, black	Small clutch, black
890	Tailored pant, stone or taupe		Basic tank, black	Casual jacket	Wedges, tan	Everyday tote bag, tan
891	Tailored pant, stone or taupe		Basic tank, black	Casual jacket	Ballet flats, black	Everyday tote bag, black
892	Tailored pant, stone or taupe		Basic tank, black	Casual jacket	Ballet flats, black	Everyday tote bag, tan
893	Tailored pant, stone or taupe		Basic tank, black	Casual jacket	Strappy heel, black	Everyday tote bag, black

	TROUSER/ PANT	SKIRT/ SHORTS/ DRESS	TOP	OUTERWEAR	SHOE	BAG
894	Tailored pant, stone or taupe		Basic tank, black	Casual jacket	Strappy heel, black	Everyday tote bag, tan
895	Tailored pant, stone or taupe		Basic tank, black	Casual jacket	Strappy heel, black	Small clutch, black
896	Tailored pant, stone or taupe		Basic tank, black	Casual jacket	Strappy heel, black	Everyday tote bag, black
897	Tailored pant, stone or taupe		Basic tank, white		Round pumps, black	Everyday tote bag, black
898	Tailored pant, stone or taupe		Basic tank, white		Round pumps, black	Everyday tote bag, tan
899	Tailored pant, stone or taupe		Basic tank, white		Round pumps, black	Small clutch, black
900	Tailored pant, stone or taupe		Basic tank, white		Wedges, tan	Everyday tote bag, tan
901	Tailored pant, stone or taupe		Basic tank, white		Ballet flats, black	Everyday tote bag, black
902	Tailored pant, stone or taupe		Basic tank, white		Ballet flats, black	Everyday tote bag, tan
903	Tailored pant, stone or taupe		Basic tank, white		Ballet flats, black	Small clutch, black
904	Tailored pant, stone or taupe		Basic tank, white		Strappy heel, black	Everyday tote bag, black
905	Tailored pant, stone or taupe		Basic tank, white		Strappy heel, black	Everyday tote bag, tan
906	Tailored pant, stone or taupe		Basic tank, white		Strappy heel, black	Small clutch, black
907	Tailored pant, stone or taupe		Basic tank, white		Dressy sandals	Everyday tote bag, tan
908	Tailored pant, stone or taupe		Basic tank, white	Parka / trench coat	Knee-high boots, black	Everyday tote bag, black
909	Tailored pant, stone or taupe		Basic tank, white	Parka / trench coat	Knee-high boots, black	Everyday tote bag, tan

	TROUSER/ PANT	SKIRT/ SHORTS/ DRESS	TOP	OUTERWEAR	SHOE	BAG
910	Tailored pant, stone or taupe		Basic tank, white	Parka / trench coat	Knee-high boots, black	Small clutch, black
911	Tailored pant, stone or taupe		Basic tank, white	Parka / trench coat	Round pumps, black	Everyday tote bag, black
912	Tailored pant, stone or taupe		Basic tank, white	Parka / trench coat	Round pumps, black	Everyday tote bag, tan
913	Tailored pant, stone or taupe		Basic tank, white	Parka / trench coat	Round pumps, black	Small clutch, black
914	Tailored pant, stone or taupe		Basic tank, white	Parka / trench coat	Wedges, tan	Everyday tote bag, tan
915	Tailored pant, stone or taupe		Basic tank, white	Parka / trench coat	Ballet flats, black	Everyday tote bag, black
916	Tailored pant, stone or taupe		Basic tank, white	Parka / trench coat	Ballet flats, black	Everyday tote bag, tan
917	Tailored pant, stone or taupe		Basic tank, white	Cardigan, black	Knee-high boots, black	Everyday tote bag, black
918	Tailored pant, stone or taupe		Basic tank, white	Cardigan, black	Knee-high boots, black	Everyday tote bag, tan
919	Tailored pant, stone or taupe		Basic tank, white	Cardigan, black	Knee-high boots, black	Small clutch, black
920	Tailored pant, stone or taupe		Basic tank, white	Cardigan, black	Round pumps, black	Everyday tote bag, black
921	Tailored pant, stone or taupe		Basic tank, white	Cardigan, black	Round pumps, black	Everyday tote bag, tan
922	Tailored pant, stone or taupe		Basic tank, white	Cardigan, black	Round pumps, black	Small clutch, black
923	Tailored pant, stone or taupe		Basic tank, white	Cardigan, black	Wedges, tan	Everyday tote bag, tan
924	Tailored pant, stone or taupe		Basic tank, white	Cardigan, black	Ballet flats, black	Everyday tote bag, black
925	Tailored pant, stone or taupe		Basic tank, white	Cardigan, black	Ballet flats, black	Everyday tote bag, tan

|---|---|---|---|---|---|---|
926	Tailored pant, stone or taupe		Basic tank, white	Cardigan, black	Strappy heel, black	Everyday tote bag, black
927	Tailored pant, stone or taupe		Basic tank, white	Cardigan, black	Strappy heel, black	Everyday tote bag, tan
928	Tailored pant, stone or taupe		Basic tank, white	Cardigan, black	Strappy heel, black	Small clutch, black
929	Tailored pant, stone or taupe		Basic tank, white	Blazer, black	Knee-high boots, black	Everyday tote bag, black
930	Tailored pant, stone or taupe		Basic tank, white	Blazer, black	Knee-high boots, black	Everyday tote bag, tan
931	Tailored pant, stone or taupe		Basic tank, white	Blazer, black	Knee-high boots, black	Small clutch, black
932	Tailored pant, stone or taupe		Basic tank, white	Blazer, black	Round pumps, black	Everyday tote bag, black
933	Tailored pant, stone or taupe		Basic tank, white	Blazer, black	Round pumps, black	Everyday tote bag, tan
934	Tailored pant, stone or taupe		Basic tank, white	Blazer, black	Round pumps, black	Small clutch, black
935	Tailored pant, stone or taupe		Basic tank, white	Blazer, black	Wedges, tan	Everyday tote bag, tan
936	Tailored pant, stone or taupe		Basic tank, white	Blazer, black	Ballet flats, black	Everyday tote bag, black
937	Tailored pant, stone or taupe		Basic tank, white	Blazer, black	Ballet flats, tan	Everyday tote bag, tan
938	Tailored pant, stone or taupe		Basic tank, white	Blazer, black	Ballet flats, black	Small clutch, black
939	Tailored pant, stone or taupe		Basic tank, white	Blazer, black	Strappy heel, black	Everyday tote bag, black
940	Tailored pant, stone or taupe		Basic tank, white	Blazer, black	Strappy heel, black	Everyday tote bag, tan
941	Tailored pant, stone or taupe		Basic tank, white	Blazer, black	Strappy heel, black	Small clutch, black

	TROUSER/PANT	SKIRT/SHORTS/DRESS	TOP	OUTERWEAR	SHOE	BAG
942	Tailored pant, stone or taupe		Basic tank, white	Blazer, stone	Knee-high boots, black	Everyday tote bag, black
943	Tailored pant, stone or taupe		Basic tank, white	Blazer, stone	Knee-high boots, black	Everyday tote bag, tan
944	Tailored pant, stone or taupe		Basic tank, white	Blazer, stone	Knee-high boots, black	Small clutch, black
945	Tailored pant, stone or taupe		Basic tank, white	Blazer, stone	Round pumps, black	Everyday tote bag, black
946	Tailored pant, stone or taupe		Basic tank, white	Blazer, stone	Round pumps, black	Everyday tote bag, tan
947	Tailored pant, stone or taupe		Basic tank, white	Blazer, stone	Round pumps, black	Small clutch, black
948	Tailored pant, stone or taupe		Basic tank, white	Blazer, stone	Wedges, tan	Everyday tote bag, tan
949	Tailored pant, stone or taupe		Basic tank, white	Blazer, stone	Ballet flats, black	Everyday tote bag, black
950	Tailored pant, stone or taupe		Basic tank, white	Blazer, stone	Ballet flats, black	Everyday tote bag, tan
951	Tailored pant, stone or taupe		Basic tank, white	Blazer, stone	Strappy heel, black	Everyday tote bag, black
952	Tailored pant, stone or taupe		Basic tank, white	Blazer, stone	Strappy heel, black	Everyday tote bag, tan
953	Tailored pant, stone or taupe		Basic tank, white	Blazer, stone	Strappy heel, black	Small clutch, black
954	Tailored pant, stone or taupe		Basic tank, white	Casual jacket	Knee-high boots, black	Everyday tote bag, black
955	Tailored pant, stone or taupe		Basic tank, white	Casual jacket	Knee-high boots, black	Everyday tote bag, tan
956	Tailored pant, stone or taupe		Basic tank, white	Casual jacket	Knee-high boots, black	Small clutch, black
957	Tailored pant, stone or taupe		Basic tank, white	Casual jacket	Round pumps, black	Everyday tote bag, black

	TROUSER/ PANT	SKIRT/ SHORTS/ DRESS	TOP	OUTERWEAR	SHOE	BAG
958	Tailored pant, stone or taupe		Basic tank, white	Casual jacket	Round pumps, black	Everyday tote bag, tan
959	Tailored pant, stone or taupe		Basic tank, white	Casual jacket	Round pumps, black	Small clutch, black
960	Tailored pant, stone or taupe		Basic tank, white	Casual jacket	Wedges, tan	Everyday tote bag, tan
961	Tailored pant, stone or taupe		Basic tank, white	Casual jacket	Ballet flats, black	Everyday tote bag, black
962	Tailored pant, stone or taupe		Basic tank, white	Casual jacket	Ballet flats, black	Everyday tote bag, tan
963	Tailored pant, stone or taupe		Basic tank, white	Casual jacket	Strappy heel, black	Everyday tote bag, black
964	Tailored pant, stone or taupe		Basic tank, white	Casual jacket	Strappy heel, black	Everyday tote bag, tan
965	Tailored pant, stone or taupe		Basic tank, white	Casual jacket	Strappy heel, black	Small clutch, black
966	Tailored pant, stone or taupe		Blouse, accent color		Round pumps, black	Everyday tote bag, black
967	Tailored pant, stone or taupe		Blouse, accent color		Round pumps, black	Small clutch, black
968	Tailored pant, stone or taupe		Blouse, accent color		Wedges, tan	Everyday tote bag, tan
969	Tailored pant, stone or taupe		Blouse, accent color		Ballet flats, black	Everyday tote bag, black
970	Tailored pant, stone or taupe		Blouse, accent color		Ballet flats, black	Everyday tote bag, tan
971	Tailored pant, stone or taupe		Blouse, accent color		Strappy heel, black	Everyday tote bag, black
972	Tailored pant, stone or taupe		Blouse, accent color		Strappy heel, black	Small clutch, black
973	Tailored pant, stone or taupe		Blouse, accent color	Parka / trench coat	Knee-high boots, black	Everyday tote bag, black

	TROUSER/ PANT	SKIRT/ SHORTS/ DRESS	TOP	OUTERWEAR	SHOE	BAG
974	Tailored pant, stone or taupe		Blouse, accent color	Parka / trench coat	Knee-high boots, black	Everyday tote bag, tan
975	Tailored pant, stone or taupe		Blouse, accent color	Parka / trench coat	Knee-high boots, black	Small clutch, black
976	Tailored pant, stone or taupe		Blouse, accent color	Parka / trench coat	Round pumps, black	Everyday tote bag, black
977	Tailored pant, stone or taupe		Blouse, accent color	Parka / trench coat	Round pumps, black	Everyday tote bag, tan
978	Tailored pant, stone or taupe		Blouse, accent color	Parka / trench coat	Round pumps, black	Small clutch, black
979	Tailored pant, stone or taupe		Blouse, accent color	Parka / trench coat	Wedges, tan	Everyday tote bag, tan
980	Tailored pant, stone or taupe		Blouse, accent color	Parka / trench coat	Ballet flats, black	Everyday tote bag, black
981	Tailored pant, stone or taupe		Blouse, accent color	Parka / trench coat	Ballet flats, black	Everyday tote bag, tan
982	Tailored pant, stone or taupe		Blouse, accent color	Parka / trench coat	Strappy heel, black	Everyday tote bag, black
983	Tailored pant, stone or taupe		Blouse, accent color	Parka / trench coat	Strappy heel, black	Everyday tote bag, tan
984	Tailored pant, stone or taupe		Blouse, accent color	Parka / trench coat	Strappy heel, black	Small clutch, black
985	Tailored pant, stone or taupe		Blouse, accent color	Cardigan, black	Knee-high boots, black	Everyday tote bag, black
986	Tailored pant, stone or taupe		Blouse, accent color	Cardigan, black	Knee-high boots, black	Everyday tote bag, tan
987	Tailored pant, stone or taupe		Blouse, accent color	Cardigan, black	Knee-high boots, black	Small clutch, black
988	Tailored pant, stone or taupe		Blouse, accent color	Cardigan, black	Round pumps, black	Everyday tote bag, black
989	Tailored pant, stone or taupe		Blouse, accent color	Cardigan, black	Round pumps, black	Everyday tote bag, tan

	TROUSER/ PANT	SKIRT/ SHORTS/ DRESS	TOP	OUTERWEAR	SHOE	BAG
990	Tailored pant, stone or taupe		Blouse, accent color	Cardigan, black	Round pumps, black	Small clutch, black
991	Tailored pant, stone or taupe		Blouse, accent color	Cardigan, black	Wedges, tan	Everyday tote bag, tan
992	Tailored pant, stone or taupe		Blouse, accent color	Cardigan, black	Ballet flats, black	Everyday tote bag, black
993	Tailored pant, stone or taupe		Blouse, accent color	Cardigan, black	Ballet flats, black	Everyday tote bag, tan
994	Tailored pant, stone or taupe		Blouse, accent color	Cardigan, black	Strappy heel, black	Everyday tote bag, black
995	Tailored pant, stone or taupe		Blouse, accent color	Cardigan, black	Strappy heel, black	Everyday tote bag, tan
996	Tailored pant, stone or taupe		Blouse, accent color	Cardigan, black	Strappy heel, black	Small clutch, black
997	Tailored pant, stone or taupe		Blouse, accent color	Blazer, black	Knee-high boots, black	Everyday tote bag, black
998	Tailored pant, stone or taupe		Blouse, accent color	Blazer, black	Knee-high boots, black	Everyday tote bag, tan
999	Tailored pant, stone or taupe		Blouse, accent color	Blazer, black	Knee-high boots, black	Small clutch, black
1000	Tailored pant, stone or taupe		Blouse, accent color	Blazer, black	Round pumps, black	Everyday tote bag, black
1001	Tailored pant, stone or taupe		Blouse, accent color	Blazer, black	Round pumps, black	Everyday tote bag, tan
1002	Tailored pant, stone or taupe		Blouse, accent color	Blazer, black	Round pumps, black	Small clutch, black
1003	Tailored pant, stone or taupe		Blouse, accent color	Blazer, black	Wedges, tan	Everyday tote bag, tan
1004	Tailored pant, stone or taupe		Blouse, accent color	Blazer, black	Ballet flats, black	Everyday tote bag, black
1005	Tailored pant, stone or taupe		Blouse, accent color	Blazer, black	Ballet flats, black	Everyday tote bag, tan

185

TROUSER/PANT	SKIRT/SHORTS/DRESS	TOP	OUTERWEAR	SHOE	BAG
1006	Tailored pant, stone or taupe		Blouse, accent color	Blazer, black	Strappy heel, black	Everyday tote bag, black
1007	Tailored pant, stone or taupe		Blouse, accent color	Blazer, black	Strappy heel, black	Everyday tote bag, tan
1008	Tailored pant, stone or taupe		Blouse, accent color	Blazer, black	Strappy heel, black	Small clutch, black
1009	Tailored pant, stone or taupe		Blouse, accent color	Blazer, stone	Knee-high boots, black	Everyday tote bag, black
1010	Tailored pant, stone or taupe		Blouse, accent color	Blazer, stone	Knee-high boots, black	Everyday tote bag, tan
1011	Tailored pant, stone or taupe		Blouse, accent color	Blazer, stone	Knee-high boots, black	Small clutch, black
1012	Tailored pant, stone or taupe		Blouse, accent color	Blazer, stone	Round pumps, black	Everyday tote bag, black
1013	Tailored pant, stone or taupe		Blouse, accent color	Blazer, stone	Round pumps, black	Everyday tote bag, tan
1014	Tailored pant, stone or taupe		Blouse, accent color	Blazer, stone	Round pumps, black	Small clutch, black
1015	Tailored pant, stone or taupe		Blouse, accent color	Blazer, stone	Wedges, tan	Everyday tote bag, tan
1016	Tailored pant, stone or taupe		Blouse, accent color	Blazer, stone	Ballet flats, black	Everyday tote bag, black
1017	Tailored pant, stone or taupe		Blouse, accent color	Blazer, stone	Ballet flats, black	Everyday tote bag, tan
1018	Tailored pant, stone or taupe		Blouse, accent color	Blazer, stone	Strappy heel, black	Everyday tote bag, black
1019	Tailored pant, stone or taupe		Blouse, accent color	Blazer, stone	Strappy heel, black	Everyday tote bag, tan
1020	Tailored pant, stone or taupe		Blouse, accent color	Blazer, stone	Strappy heel, black	Small clutch, black
1021	Tailored pant, stone or taupe		Blouse, accent color	Casual jacket	Knee-high boots, black	Everyday tote bag, black

	TROUSER/ PANT	SKIRT/ SHORTS/ DRESS	TOP	OUTERWEAR	SHOE	BAG
1022	Tailored pant, stone or taupe		Blouse, accent color	Casual jacket	Knee-high boots, black	Everyday tote bag, tan
1023	Tailored pant, stone or taupe		Blouse, accent color	Casual jacket	Knee-high boots, black	Small clutch, black
1024	Tailored pant, stone or taupe		Blouse, accent color	Casual jacket	Round pumps, black	Everyday tote bag, black
1025	Tailored pant, stone or taupe		Blouse, accent color	Casual jacket	Round pumps, black	Everyday tote bag, tan
1026	Tailored pant, stone or taupe		Blouse, accent color	Casual jacket	Round pumps, black	Small clutch, black
1027	Tailored pant, stone or taupe		Blouse, accent color	Casual jacket	Wedges, tan	Everyday tote bag, tan
1028	Tailored pant, stone or taupe		Blouse, accent color	Casual jacket	Ballet flats, black	Everyday tote bag, black
1029	Tailored pant, stone or taupe		Blouse, accent color	Casual jacket	Ballet flats, black	Everyday tote bag, tan
1030	Tailored pant, stone or taupe		Blouse, accent color	Casual jacket	Strappy heel, black	Everyday tote bag, black
1031	Tailored pant, stone or taupe		Blouse, accent color	Casual jacket	Strappy heel, black	Everyday tote bag, tan
1032	Tailored pant, stone or taupe		Blouse, accent color	Casual jacket	Strappy heel, black	Small clutch, black
1033	Tailored pant, stone or taupe		Second blouse, accent color		Round pumps, black	Everyday tote bag, black
1034	Tailored pant, stone or taupe		Second blouse, accent color		Round pumps, black	Small clutch, black
1035	Tailored pant, stone or taupe		Second blouse, accent color		Wedges, tan	Everyday tote bag, tan
1036	Tailored pant, stone or taupe		Second blouse, accent color		Ballet flats, black	Everyday tote bag, black
1037	Tailored pant, stone or taupe		Second blouse, accent color		Ballet flats, black	Everyday tote bag, tan

	TROUSER/PANT	SKIRT/SHORTS/DRESS	TOP	OUTERWEAR	SHOE	BAG
1038	Tailored pant, stone or taupe		Second blouse, accent color		Strappy heel, black	Everyday tote bag, black
1039	Tailored pant, stone or taupe		Second blouse, accent color		Strappy heel, black	Small clutch, black
1040	Tailored pant, stone or taupe		Second blouse, accent color	Parka / trench coat	Knee-high boots, black	Everyday tote bag, black
1041	Tailored pant, stone or taupe		Second blouse, accent color	Parka / trench coat	Knee-high boots, black	Everyday tote bag, tan
1042	Tailored pant, stone or taupe		Second blouse, accent color	Parka / trench coat	Knee-high boots, black	Small clutch, black
1043	Tailored pant, stone or taupe		Second blouse, accent color	Parka / trench coat	Round pumps, black	Everyday tote bag, black
1044	Tailored pant, stone or taupe		Second blouse, accent color	Parka / trench coat	Round pumps, black	Everyday tote bag, tan
1045	Tailored pant, stone or taupe		Second blouse, accent color	Parka / trench coat	Round pumps, black	Small clutch, black
1046	Tailored pant, stone or taupe		Second blouse, accent color	Parka / trench coat	Wedges, tan	Everyday tote bag, tan
1047	Tailored pant, stone or taupe		Second blouse, accent color	Parka / trench coat	Ballet flats, black	Everyday tote bag, black
1048	Tailored pant, stone or taupe		Second blouse, accent color	Parka / trench coat	Ballet flats, black	Everyday tote bag, tan
1049	Tailored pant, stone or taupe		Second blouse, accent color	Cardigan, black	Knee-high boots, black	Everyday tote bag, black
1050	Tailored pant, stone or taupe		Second blouse, accent color	Cardigan, black	Knee-high boots, black	Everyday tote bag, tan
1051	Tailored pant, stone or taupe		Second blouse, accent color	Cardigan, black	Knee-high boots, black	Small clutch, black
1052	Tailored pant, stone or taupe		Second blouse, accent color	Cardigan, black	Round pumps, black	Everyday tote bag, black
1053	Tailored pant, stone or taupe		Second blouse, accent color	Cardigan, black	Round pumps, black	Everyday tote bag, tan

	TROUSER/ PANT	SKIRT/ SHORTS/ DRESS	TOP	OUTERWEAR	SHOE	BAG
1054	Tailored pant, stone or taupe		Second blouse, accent color	Cardigan, black	Round pumps, black	Small clutch, black
1055	Tailored pant, stone or taupe		Second blouse, accent color	Cardigan, black	Wedges, tan	Everyday tote bag, tan
1056	Tailored pant, stone or taupe		Second blouse, accent color	Cardigan, black	Ballet flats, black	Everyday tote bag, black
1057	Tailored pant, stone or taupe		Second blouse, accent color	Cardigan, black	Ballet flats, black	Everyday tote bag, tan
1058	Tailored pant, stone or taupe		Second blouse, accent color	Cardigan, black	Strappy heel, black	Everyday tote bag, black
1059	Tailored pant, stone or taupe		Second blouse, accent color	Cardigan, black	Strappy heel, black	Everyday tote bag, tan
1060	Tailored pant, stone or taupe		Second blouse, accent color	Cardigan, black	Strappy heel, black	Small clutch, black
1061	Tailored pant, stone or taupe		Second blouse, accent color	Blazer, black	Knee-high boots, black	Everyday tote bag, black
1062	Tailored pant, stone or taupe		Second blouse, accent color	Blazer, black	Knee-high boots, black	Everyday tote bag, tan
1063	Tailored pant, stone or taupe		Second blouse, accent color	Blazer, black	Knee-high boots, black	Small clutch, black
1064	Tailored pant, stone or taupe		Second blouse, accent color	Blazer, black	Round pumps, black	Everyday tote bag, black
1065	Tailored pant, stone or taupe		Second blouse, accent color	Blazer, black	Round pumps, black	Everyday tote bag, tan
1066	Tailored pant, stone or taupe		Second blouse, accent color	Blazer, black	Round pumps, black	Small clutch, black
1067	Tailored pant, stone or taupe		Second blouse, accent color	Blazer, black	Wedges, tan	Everyday tote bag, tan
1068	Tailored pant, stone or taupe		Second blouse, accent color	Blazer, black	Ballet flats, black	Everyday tote bag, black
1069	Tailored pant, stone or taupe		Second blouse, accent color	Blazer, black	Ballet flats, black	Everyday tote bag, tan

	TROUSER/ PANT	SKIRT/ SHORTS/ DRESS	TOP	OUTERWEAR	SHOE	BAG
1070	Tailored pant, stone or taupe		Second blouse, accent color	Blazer, black	Strappy heel, black	Everyday tote bag, black
1071	Tailored pant, stone or taupe		Second blouse, accent color	Blazer, black	Strappy heel, black	Everyday tote bag, tan
1072	Tailored pant, stone or taupe		Second blouse, accent color	Blazer, black	Strappy heel, black	Small clutch, black
1073	Tailored pant, stone or taupe		Second blouse, accent color	Blazer, stone	Knee-high boots, black	Everyday tote bag, black
1074	Tailored pant, stone or taupe		Second blouse, accent color	Blazer, stone	Knee-high boots, black	Everyday tote bag, tan
1075	Tailored pant, stone or taupe		Second blouse, accent color	Blazer, stone	Knee-high boots, black	Small clutch, black
1076	Tailored pant, stone or taupe		Second blouse, accent color	Blazer, stone	Round pumps, black	Everyday tote bag, black
1077	Tailored pant, stone or taupe		Second blouse, accent color	Blazer, stone	Round pumps, black	Everyday tote bag, tan
1078	Tailored pant, stone or taupe		Second blouse, accent color	Blazer, stone	Round pumps, black	Small clutch, black
1079	Tailored pant, stone or taupe		Second blouse, accent color	Blazer, stone	Wedges, tan	Everyday tote bag, tan
1080	Tailored pant, stone or taupe		Second blouse, accent color	Blazer, stone	Ballet flats, black	Everyday tote bag, black
1081	Tailored pant, stone or taupe		Second blouse, accent color	Blazer, stone	Ballet flats, black	Everyday tote bag, tan
1082	Tailored pant, stone or taupe		Second blouse, accent color	Blazer, stone	Strappy heel, black	Everyday tote bag, black
1083	Tailored pant, stone or taupe		Second blouse, accent color	Blazer, stone	Strappy heel, black	Everyday tote bag, tan
1084	Tailored pant, stone or taupe		Second blouse, accent color	Blazer, stone	Strappy heel, black	Small clutch, black
1085	Tailored pant, stone or taupe		Second blouse, accent color	Casual jacket	Knee-high boots, black	Everyday tote bag, black

	TROUSER/ PANT	SKIRT/ SHORTS/ DRESS	TOP	OUTERWEAR	SHOE	BAG
1086	Tailored pant, stone or taupe		Second blouse, accent color	Casual jacket	Knee-high boots, black	Everyday tote bag, tan
1087	Tailored pant, stone or taupe		Second blouse, accent color	Casual jacket	Knee-high boots, black	Small clutch, black
1088	Tailored pant, stone or taupe		Second blouse, accent color	Casual jacket	Round pumps, black	Everyday tote bag, black
1089	Tailored pant, stone or taupe		Second blouse, accent color	Casual jacket	Round pumps, black	Everyday tote bag, tan
1090	Tailored pant, stone or taupe		Second blouse, accent color	Casual jacket	Round pumps, black	Small clutch, black
1091	Tailored pant, stone or taupe		Second blouse, accent color	Casual jacket	Wedges, tan	Everyday tote bag, tan
1092	Tailored pant, stone or taupe		Second blouse, accent color	Casual jacket	Ballet flats, black	Everyday tote bag, black
1093	Tailored pant, stone or taupe		Second blouse, accent color	Casual jacket	Ballet flats, black	Everyday tote bag, tan
1094	Tailored pant, stone or taupe		Second blouse, accent color	Casual jacket	Strappy heel, black	Everyday tote bag, black
1095	Tailored pant, stone or taupe		Second blouse, accent color	Casual jacket	Strappy heel, black	Everyday tote bag, tan
1096	Tailored pant, stone or taupe		Second blouse, accent color	Casual jacket	Strappy heel, black	Small clutch, black
1097	Tailored pant, stone or taupe		Three-quarter sleeved top, accent color		Round pumps, black	Everyday tote bag, black
1098	Tailored pant, stone or taupe		Three-quarter sleeved top, accent color		Round pumps, black	Everyday tote bag, tan
1099	Tailored pant, stone or taupe		Three-quarter sleeved top, accent color		Round pumps, black	Small clutch, black
1100	Tailored pant, stone or taupe		Three-quarter sleeved top, accent color		Wedges, tan	Everyday tote bag, tan
1101	Tailored pant, stone or taupe		Three-quarter sleeved top, accent color		Ballet flats, black	Everyday tote bag, black

	TROUSER/PANT	SKIRT/SHORTS/DRESS	TOP	OUTERWEAR	SHOE	BAG
1102	Tailored pant, stone or taupe		Three-quarter sleeved top, accent color		Ballet flats, black	Everyday tote bag, tan
1103	Tailored pant, stone or taupe		Three-quarter sleeved top, accent color		Ballet flats, black	Small clutch, black
1104	Tailored pant, stone or taupe		Three-quarter sleeved top, accent color		Strappy heel, black	Everyday tote bag, black
1105	Tailored pant, stone or taupe		Three-quarter sleeved top, accent color		Strappy heel, black	Everyday tote bag, tan
1106	Tailored pant, stone or taupe		Three-quarter sleeved top, accent color		Strappy heel, black	Small clutch, black
1107	Tailored pant, stone or taupe		Three-quarter sleeved top, accent color	Parka / trench coat	Knee-high boots, black	Everyday tote bag, black
1108	Tailored pant, stone or taupe		Three-quarter sleeved top, accent color	Parka / trench coat	Knee-high boots, black	Everyday tote bag, tan
1109	Tailored pant, stone or taupe		Three-quarter sleeved top, accent color	Parka / trench coat	Round pumps, black	Everyday tote bag, black
1110	Tailored pant, stone or taupe		Three-quarter sleeved top, accent color	Parka / trench coat	Round pumps, black	Everyday tote bag, tan
1111	Tailored pant, stone or taupe		Three-quarter sleeved top, accent color	Parka / trench coat	Round pumps, black	Small clutch, black
1112	Tailored pant, stone or taupe		Three-quarter sleeved top, accent color	Parka / trench coat	Wedges, tan	Everyday tote bag, tan
1113	Tailored pant, stone or taupe		Three-quarter sleeved top, accent color	Parka / trench coat	Ballet flats, black	Everyday tote bag, black
1114	Tailored pant, stone or taupe		Three-quarter sleeved top, accent color	Parka / trench coat	Ballet flats, black	Everyday tote bag, tan
1115	Tailored pant, stone or taupe		Three-quarter sleeved top, accent color	Blazer, black	Knee-high boots, black	Everyday tote bag, black
1116	Tailored pant, stone or taupe		Three-quarter sleeved top, accent color	Blazer, black	Knee-high boots, black	Everyday tote bag, tan

	TROUSER/PANT	SKIRT/SHORTS/DRESS	TOP	OUTERWEAR	SHOE	BAG
1117	Tailored pant, stone or taupe		Three-quarter sleeved top, accent color	Blazer, black	Knee-high boots, black	Small clutch, black
1118	Tailored pant, stone or taupe		Three-quarter sleeved top, accent color	Blazer, black	Round pumps, black	Everyday tote bag, black
1119	Tailored pant, stone or taupe		Three-quarter sleeved top, accent color	Blazer, black	Round pumps, black	Everyday tote bag, tan
1120	Tailored pant, stone or taupe		Three-quarter sleeved top, accent color	Blazer, black	Round pumps, black	Small clutch, black
1121	Tailored pant, stone or taupe		Three-quarter sleeved top, accent color	Blazer, black	Wedges, tan	Everyday tote bag, tan
1122	Tailored pant, stone or taupe		Three-quarter sleeved top, accent color	Blazer, black	Ballet flats, black	Everyday tote bag, black
1123	Tailored pant, stone or taupe		Three-quarter sleeved top, accent color	Blazer, black	Ballet flats, black	Everyday tote bag, tan
1124	Tailored pant, stone or taupe		Three-quarter sleeved top, accent color	Blazer, black	Strappy heel, tan	Everyday tote bag, black
1125	Tailored pant, stone or taupe		Three-quarter sleeved top, accent color	Blazer, black	Strappy heel, black	Everyday tote bag, tan
1126	Tailored pant, stone or taupe		Three-quarter sleeved top, accent color	Blazer, black	Strappy heel, black	Small clutch, black
1127	Tailored pant, stone or taupe		Three-quarter sleeved top, accent color	Blazer, stone	Knee-high boots, black	Everyday tote bag, black
1128	Tailored pant, stone or taupe		Three-quarter sleeved top, accent color	Blazer, stone	Knee-high boots, black	Everyday tote bag, tan
1129	Tailored pant, stone or taupe		Three-quarter sleeved top, accent color	Blazer, stone	Knee-high boots, black	Small clutch, black
1130	Tailored pant, stone or taupe		Three-quarter sleeved top, accent color	Blazer, stone	Round pumps, black	Everyday tote bag, black
1131	Tailored pant, stone or taupe		Three-quarter sleeved top, accent color	Blazer, stone	Round pumps, black	Everyday tote bag, tan

	TROUSER/ PANT	SKIRT/ SHORTS/ DRESS	TOP	OUTERWEAR	SHOE	BAG
1132	Tailored pant, stone or taupe		Three-quarter sleeved top, accent color	Blazer, stone	Round pumps, black	Small clutch, black
1133	Tailored pant, stone or taupe		Three-quarter sleeved top, accent color	Blazer, stone	Wedges, tan	Everyday tote bag, tan
1134	Tailored pant, stone or taupe		Three-quarter sleeved top, accent color	Blazer, stone	Ballet flats, black	Everyday tote bag, black
1135	Tailored pant, stone or taupe		Three-quarter sleeved top, accent color	Blazer, stone	Ballet flats, black	Everyday tote bag, tan
1136	Tailored pant, stone or taupe		Three-quarter sleeved top, accent color	Blazer, stone	Strappy heel, black	Everyday tote bag, black
1137	Tailored pant, stone or taupe		Three-quarter sleeved top, accent color	Blazer, stone	Strappy heel, black	Everyday tote bag, tan
1138	Tailored pant, stone or taupe		Three-quarter sleeved top, accent color	Blazer, stone	Strappy heel, black	Small clutch, black
1139	Tailored pant, stone or taupe		Three-quarter sleeved top, accent color	Casual jacket	Knee-high boots, black	Everyday tote bag, black
1140	Tailored pant, stone or taupe		Three-quarter sleeved top, accent color	Casual jacket	Knee-high boots, black	Everyday tote bag, tan
1141	Tailored pant, stone or taupe		Three-quarter sleeved top, accent color	Casual jacket	Knee-high boots, black	Small clutch, black
1142	Tailored pant, stone or taupe		Three-quarter sleeved top, accent color	Casual jacket	Round pumps, black	Everyday tote bag, black
1143	Tailored pant, stone or taupe		Three-quarter sleeved top, accent color	Casual jacket	Round pumps, black	Everyday tote bag, tan
1144	Tailored pant, stone or taupe		Three-quarter sleeved top, accent color	Casual jacket	Round pumps, black	Small clutch, black
1145	Tailored pant, stone or taupe		Three-quarter sleeved top, accent color	Casual jacket	Wedges, tan	Everyday tote bag, tan
1146	Tailored pant, stone or taupe		Three-quarter sleeved top, accent color	Casual jacket	Ballet flats, black	Everyday tote bag, black

	TROUSER/ PANT	SKIRT/ SHORTS/ DRESS	TOP	OUTERWEAR	SHOE	BAG
1147	Tailored pant, stone or taupe		Three-quarter sleeved top, accent color	Casual jacket	Ballet flats, black	Everyday tote bag, tan
1148	Tailored pant, stone or taupe		Three-quarter sleeved top, accent color	Casual jacket	Strappy heel, black	Everyday tote bag, black
1149	Tailored pant, stone or taupe		Three-quarter sleeved top, accent color	Casual jacket	Strappy heel, black	Everyday tote bag, tan
1150	Tailored pant, stone or taupe		Three-quarter sleeved top, accent color	Casual jacket	Strappy heel, black	Small clutch, black
1151	Tailored pant, stone or taupe		Three-quarter sleeved top, black		Round pumps, black	Everyday tote bag, black
1152	Tailored pant, stone or taupe		Three-quarter sleeved top, black		Round pumps, black	Everyday tote bag, tan
1153	Tailored pant, stone or taupe		Three-quarter sleeved top, black		Round pumps, black	Small clutch, black
1154	Tailored pant, stone or taupe		Three-quarter sleeved top, black		Wedges, tan	Everyday tote bag, tan
1155	Tailored pant, stone or taupe		Three-quarter sleeved top, black		Ballet flats, black	Everyday tote bag, black
1156	Tailored pant, stone or taupe		Three-quarter sleeved top, black		Ballet flats, black	Everyday tote bag, tan
1157	Tailored pant, stone or taupe		Three-quarter sleeved top, black		Ballet flats, black	Small clutch, black
1158	Tailored pant, stone or taupe		Three-quarter sleeved top, black		Strappy heel, black	Everyday tote bag, black
1159	Tailored pant, stone or taupe		Three-quarter sleeved top, black		Strappy heel, black	Small clutch, black
1160	Tailored pant, stone or taupe		Three-quarter sleeved top, black	Parka / trench coat	Knee-high boots, black	Everyday tote bag, black
1161	Tailored pant, stone or taupe		Three-quarter sleeved top, black	Parka / trench coat	Knee-high boots, black	Everyday tote bag, tan

	TROUSER/ PANT	SKIRT/ SHORTS/ DRESS	TOP	OUTERWEAR	SHOE	BAG
1162	Tailored pant, stone or taupe		Three-quarter sleeved top, black	Parka / trench coat	Round pumps, black	Everyday tote bag, black
1163	Tailored pant, stone or taupe		Three-quarter sleeved top, black	Parka / trench coat	Round pumps, black	Everyday tote bag, tan
1164	Tailored pant, stone or taupe		Three-quarter sleeved top, black	Parka / trench coat	Round pumps, black	Small clutch, black
1165	Tailored pant, stone or taupe		Three-quarter sleeved top, black	Parka / trench coat	Wedges, tan	Everyday tote bag, tan
1166	Tailored pant, stone or taupe		Three-quarter sleeved top, black	Parka / trench coat	Ballet flats, black	Everyday tote bag, black
1167	Tailored pant, stone or taupe		Three-quarter sleeved top, black	Parka / trench coat	Ballet flats, black	Everyday tote bag, tan
1168	Tailored pant, stone or taupe		Three-quarter sleeved top, black	Blazer, black	Knee-high boots, black	Everyday tote bag, black
1169	Tailored pant, stone or taupe		Three-quarter sleeved top, black	Blazer, black	Knee-high boots, black	Everyday tote bag, tan
1170	Tailored pant, stone or taupe		Three-quarter sleeved top, black	Blazer, black	Knee-high boots, black	Small clutch, black
1171	Tailored pant, stone or taupe		Three-quarter sleeved top, black	Blazer, black	Round pumps, black	Everyday tote bag, black
1172	Tailored pant, stone or taupe		Three-quarter sleeved top, black	Blazer, black	Round pumps, black	Everyday tote bag, tan
1173	Tailored pant, stone or taupe		Three-quarter sleeved top, black	Blazer, black	Round pumps, black	Small clutch, black
1174	Tailored pant, stone or taupe		Three-quarter sleeved top, black	Blazer, black	Wedges, tan	Everyday tote bag, tan
1175	Tailored pant, stone or taupe		Three-quarter sleeved top, black	Blazer, black	Ballet flats, black	Everyday tote bag, black
1176	Tailored pant, stone or taupe		Three-quarter sleeved top, black	Blazer, black	Ballet flats, black	Everyday tote bag, tan
1177	Tailored pant, stone or taupe		Three-quarter sleeved top, black	Blazer, black	Strappy heel, black	Everyday tote bag, black

	TROUSER/ PANT	SKIRT/ SHORTS/ DRESS	TOP	OUTERWEAR	SHOE	BAG
1178	Tailored pant, stone or taupe		Three-quarter sleeved top, black	Blazer, black	Strappy heel, black	Everyday tote bag, tan
1179	Tailored pant, stone or taupe		Three-quarter sleeved top, black	Blazer, black	Strappy heel, black	Small clutch, black
1180	Tailored pant, stone or taupe		Three-quarter sleeved top, black	Blazer, stone	Knee-high boots, black	Everyday tote bag, black
1181	Tailored pant, stone or taupe		Three-quarter sleeved top, black	Blazer, stone	Knee-high boots, black	Everyday tote bag, tan
1182	Tailored pant, stone or taupe		Three-quarter sleeved top, black	Blazer, stone	Knee-high boots, black	Small clutch, black
1183	Tailored pant, stone or taupe		Three-quarter sleeved top, black	Blazer, stone	Round pumps, black	Everyday tote bag, black
1184	Tailored pant, stone or taupe		Three-quarter sleeved top, black	Blazer, stone	Round pumps, black	Everyday tote bag, tan
1185	Tailored pant, stone or taupe		Three-quarter sleeved top, black	Blazer, stone	Round pumps, black	Small clutch, black
1186	Tailored pant, stone or taupe		Three-quarter sleeved top, black	Blazer, stone	Wedges, tan	Everyday tote bag, tan
1187	Tailored pant, stone or taupe		Three-quarter sleeved top, black	Blazer, stone	Ballet flats, black	Everyday tote bag, black
1188	Tailored pant, stone or taupe		Three-quarter sleeved top, black	Blazer, stone	Ballet flats, black	Everyday tote bag, tan
1189	Tailored pant, stone or taupe		Three-quarter sleeved top, black	Blazer, stone	Strappy heel, black	Everyday tote bag, black
1190	Tailored pant, stone or taupe		Three-quarter sleeved top, black	Blazer, stone	Strappy heel, black	Everyday tote bag, tan
1191	Tailored pant, stone or taupe		Three-quarter sleeved top, black	Blazer, stone	Strappy heel, black	Small clutch, black
1192	Tailored pant, stone or taupe		Three-quarter sleeved top, black	Casual jacket	Knee-high boots, black	Everyday tote bag, black
1193	Tailored pant, stone or taupe		Three-quarter sleeved top, black	Casual jacket	Knee-high boots, black	Everyday tote bag, tan

	TROUSER/ PANT	SKIRT/ SHORTS/ DRESS	TOP	OUTERWEAR	SHOE	BAG
1194	Tailored pant, stone or taupe		Three-quarter sleeved top, black	Casual jacket	Knee-high boots, black	Small clutch, black
1195	Tailored pant, stone or taupe		Three-quarter sleeved top, black	Casual jacket	Round pumps, black	Everyday tote bag, black
1196	Tailored pant, stone or taupe		Three-quarter sleeved top, black	Casual jacket	Round pumps, black	Everyday tote bag, tan
1197	Tailored pant, stone or taupe		Three-quarter sleeved top, black	Casual jacket	Round pumps, black	Small clutch, black
1198	Tailored pant, stone or taupe		Three-quarter sleeved top, black	Casual jacket	Wedges, tan	Everyday tote bag, tan
1199	Tailored pant, stone or taupe		Three-quarter sleeved top, black	Casual jacket	Ballet flats, black	Everyday tote bag, black
1200	Tailored pant, stone or taupe		Three-quarter sleeved top, black	Casual jacket	Ballet flats, black	Everyday tote bag, tan
1201	Tailored pant, stone or taupe		Three-quarter sleeved top, black	Casual jacket	Strappy heel, black	Everyday tote bag, black
1202	Tailored pant, stone or taupe		Three-quarter sleeved top, black	Casual jacket	Strappy heel, black	Everyday tote bag, tan
1203	Tailored pant, stone or taupe		Three-quarter sleeved top, black	Casual jacket	Strappy heel, black	Small clutch, black
1204		Casual skirt, denim	Basic tank, black		Wedges, tan	Everyday tote bag, tan
1205		Casual skirt, denim	Basic tank, black		Ballet flats, black	Everyday tote bag, black
1206		Casual skirt, denim	Basic tank, black		Dressy sandals	Everyday tote bag, tan
1207		Casual skirt, denim	Basic tank, black	Parka / trench coat	Knee-high boots, black	Everyday tote bag, black
1208		Casual skirt, denim	Basic tank, black	Parka / trench coat	Wedges, tan	Everyday tote bag, tan
1209		Casual skirt, denim	Basic tank, black	Parka / trench coat	Ballet flats, black	Everyday tote bag, black

	TROUSER/ PANT	SKIRT/ SHORTS/ DRESS	TOP	OUTERWEAR	SHOE	BAG
1210		Casual skirt, denim	Basic tank, black	Cardigan, black	Knee-high boots, black	Everyday tote bag, black
1211		Casual skirt, denim	Basic tank, black	Cardigan, black	Wedges, tan	Everyday tote bag, tan
1212		Casual skirt, denim	Basic tank, black	Cardigan, black	Ballet flats, black	Everyday tote bag, black
1213		Casual skirt, denim	Basic tank, black	Cardigan, black	Dressy sandals	Everyday tote bag, black
1214		Casual skirt, denim	Basic tank, black	Cardigan, black	Dressy sandals	Everyday tote bag, tan
1215		Casual skirt, denim	Basic tank, black	Blazer, black	Knee-high boots, black	Everyday tote bag, black
1216		Casual skirt, denim	Basic tank, black	Blazer, black	Wedges, tan	Everyday tote bag, tan
1217		Casual skirt, denim	Basic tank, black	Blazer, black	Strappy heel, black	Everyday tote bag, black
1218		Casual skirt, denim	Basic tank, black	Blazer, black	Strappy heel, black	Small clutch, black
1219		Casual skirt, denim	Basic tank, black	Blazer, stone	Wedges, tan	Everyday tote bag, tan
1220		Casual skirt, denim	Basic tank, black	Blazer, stone	Strappy heel, black	Everyday tote bag, black
1221		Casual skirt, denim	Basic tank, black	Blazer, stone	Strappy heel, black	Small clutch, black
1222		Casual skirt, denim	Basic tank, black	Casual jacket	Wedges, tan	Everyday tote bag, tan
1223		Casual skirt, denim	Basic tank, black	Casual jacket	Ballet flats, black	Everyday tote bag, black
1224		Casual skirt, denim	Basic tank, black	Casual jacket	Dressy sandals	Everyday tote bag, tan
1225		Casual skirt, denim	Basic tank, white		Wedges, tan	Everyday tote bag, tan

TROUSER/PANT	SKIRT/SHORTS/DRESS	TOP	OUTERWEAR	SHOE	BAG
1226	Casual skirt, denim	Basic tank, white		Ballet flats, black	Everyday tote bag, black
1227	Casual skirt, denim	Basic tank, white		Dressy sandals	Everyday tote bag, tan
1228	Casual skirt, denim	Basic tank, white	Parka / trench coat	Knee-high boots, black	Everyday tote bag, black
1229	Casual skirt, denim	Basic tank, white	Parka / trench coat	Wedges, tan	Everyday tote bag, tan
1230	Casual skirt, denim	Basic tank, white	Parka / trench coat	Ballet flats, black	Everyday tote bag, black
1231	Casual skirt, denim	Basic tank, white	Cardigan, black	Knee-high boots, black	Everyday tote bag, black
1232	Casual skirt, denim	Basic tank, white	Cardigan, black	Wedges, tan	Everyday tote bag, tan
1233	Casual skirt, denim	Basic tank, white	Cardigan, black	Ballet flats, black	Everyday tote bag, black
1234	Casual skirt, denim	Basic tank, white	Cardigan, black	Dressy sandals	Everyday tote bag, black
1235	Casual skirt, denim	Basic tank, white	Cardigan, black	Dressy sandals	Everyday tote bag, tan
1236	Casual skirt, denim	Basic tank, white	Blazer, black	Knee-high boots, black	Everyday tote bag, black
1237	Casual skirt, denim	Basic tank, white	Blazer, black	Wedges, tan	Everyday tote bag, tan
1238	Casual skirt, denim	Basic tank, white	Blazer, black	Strappy heel, black	Everyday tote bag, black
1239	Casual skirt, denim	Basic tank, white	Blazer, black	Strappy heel, black	Small clutch, black
1240	Casual skirt, denim	Basic tank, white	Blazer, stone	Wedges, tan	Everyday tote bag, tan

	TROUSER/ PANT	SKIRT/ SHORTS/ DRESS	TOP	OUTERWEAR	SHOE	BAG
1241		Casual skirt, denim	Basic tank, white	Casual jacket	Wedges, tan	Everyday tote bag, tan
1242		Casual skirt, denim	Basic tank, white	Casual jacket	Ballet flats, black	Everyday tote bag, black
1243		Casual skirt, denim	Basic tank, white	Casual jacket	Dressy sandals	Everyday tote bag, tan
1244		Casual skirt, denim	Blouse, accent color		Wedges, tan	Everyday tote bag, tan
1245		Casual skirt, denim	Blouse, accent color		Ballet flats, black	Everyday tote bag, black
1246		Casual skirt, denim	Blouse, accent color		Dressy sandals	Everyday tote bag, tan
1247		Casual skirt, denim	Blouse, accent color	Parka / trench coat	Knee-high boots, black	Everyday tote bag, black
1248		Casual skirt, denim	Blouse, accent color	Parka / trench coat	Wedges, tan	Everyday tote bag, tan
1249		Casual skirt, denim	Blouse, accent color	Parka / trench coat	Ballet flats, black	Everyday tote bag, black
1250		Casual skirt, denim	Blouse, accent color	Cardigan, black	Knee-high boots, black	Everyday tote bag, black
1251		Casual skirt, denim	Blouse, accent color	Cardigan, black	Wedges, tan	Everyday tote bag, tan
1252		Casual skirt, denim	Blouse, accent color	Cardigan, black	Ballet flats, black	Everyday tote bag, black
1253		Casual skirt, denim	Blouse, accent color	Cardigan, black	Dressy sandals	Everyday tote bag, black
1254		Casual skirt, denim	Blouse, accent color	Cardigan, black	Dressy sandals	Everyday tote bag, tan
1255		Casual skirt, denim	Blouse, accent color	Blazer, black	Knee-high boots, black	Everyday tote bag, black

	TROUSER/ PANT	SKIRT/ SHORTS/ DRESS	TOP	OUTERWEAR	SHOE	BAG
1256		Casual skirt, denim	Blouse, accent color	Blazer, black	Wedges, tan	Everyday tote bag, tan
1257		Casual skirt, denim	Blouse, accent color	Blazer, black	Strappy heel, black	Everyday tote bag, black
1258		Casual skirt, denim	Blouse, accent color	Blazer, black	Strappy heel, black	Small clutch, black
1259		Casual skirt, denim	Blouse, accent color	Blazer, stone	Wedges, tan	Everyday tote bag, tan
1260		Casual skirt, denim	Blouse, accent color	Casual jacket	Wedges, tan	Everyday tote bag, tan
1261		Casual skirt, denim	Blouse, accent color	Casual jacket	Ballet flats, black	Everyday tote bag, black
1262		Casual skirt, denim	Blouse, accent color	Casual jacket	Dressy sandals	Everyday tote bag, tan
1263		Casual skirt, denim	Second blouse, accent color		Wedges, tan	Everyday tote bag, tan
1264		Casual skirt, denim	Second blouse, accent color		Ballet flats, black	Everyday tote bag, black
1265		Casual skirt, denim	Second blouse, accent color		Dressy sandals	Everyday tote bag, tan
1266		Casual skirt, denim	Second blouse, accent color	Parka / trench coat	Knee-high boots, black	Everyday tote bag, black
1267		Casual skirt, denim	Second blouse, accent color	Parka / trench coat	Wedges, tan	Everyday tote bag, tan
1268		Casual skirt, denim	Second blouse, accent color	Parka / trench coat	Ballet flats, black	Everyday tote bag, black
1269		Casual skirt, denim	Second blouse, accent color	Cardigan, black	Knee-high boots, black	Everyday tote bag, black
1270		Casual skirt, denim	Second blouse, accent color	Cardigan, black	Wedges, tan	Everyday tote bag, tan

TROUSER/ PANT	SKIRT/ SHORTS/ DRESS	TOP	OUTERWEAR	SHOE	BAG
1271	Casual skirt, denim	Second blouse, accent color	Cardigan, black	Ballet flats, black	Everyday tote bag, black
1272	Casual skirt, denim	Second blouse, accent color	Cardigan, black	Dressy sandals	Everyday tote bag, black
1273	Casual skirt, denim	Second blouse, accent color	Cardigan, black	Dressy sandals	Everyday tote bag, tan
1274	Casual skirt, denim	Second blouse, accent color	Blazer, black	Knee-high boots, black	Everyday tote bag, black
1275	Casual skirt, denim	Second blouse, accent color	Blazer, black	Wedges, tan	Everyday tote bag, tan
1276	Casual skirt, denim	Second blouse, accent color	Blazer, black	Strappy heel, black	Everyday tote bag, black
1277	Casual skirt, denim	Second blouse, accent color	Blazer, black	Strappy heel, black	Small clutch, black
1278	Casual skirt, denim	Second blouse, accent color	Blazer, stone	Wedges, tan	Everyday tote bag, tan
1279	Casual skirt, denim	Second blouse, accent color	Casual jacket	Wedges, tan	Everyday tote bag, tan
1280	Casual skirt, denim	Second blouse, accent color	Casual jacket	Ballet flats, black	Everyday tote bag, black
1281	Casual skirt, denim	Second blouse, accent color	Casual jacket	Dressy sandals	Everyday tote bag, tan
1282	Casual skirt, denim	Three-quarter sleeved top, black		Ballet flats, black	Everyday tote bag, black
1283	Casual skirt, denim	Three-quarter sleeved top, black		Wedges, tan	Everyday tote bag, tan
1284	Casual skirt, denim	Three-quarter sleeved top, black		Strappy heel, black	Everyday tote bag, black
1285	Casual skirt, denim	Three-quarter sleeved top, black		Strappy heel, black	Small clutch, black

	TROUSER/PANT	SKIRT/SHORTS/DRESS	TOP	OUTERWEAR	SHOE	BAG
1286		Casual skirt, denim	Three-quarter sleeved top, black		Wedges, tan	Everyday tote bag, tan
1287		Casual skirt, denim	Three-quarter sleeved top, black		Ballet flats, black	Everyday tote bag, black
1288		Casual skirt, denim	Three-quarter sleeved top, black		Dressy sandals	Everyday tote bag, tan
1289		Casual skirt, denim	Three-quarter sleeved top, black	Parka / trench coat	Ballet flats, black	Everyday tote bag, black
1290		Casual skirt, denim	Three-quarter sleeved top, black	Parka / trench coat	Knee-high boots, black	Everyday tote bag, black
1291		Casual skirt, denim	Three-quarter sleeved top, black	Blazer, black	Knee-high boots, black	Everyday tote bag, black
1292		Casual skirt, denim	Three-quarter sleeved top, black	Blazer, black	Wedges, tan	Everyday tote bag, tan
1293		Casual skirt, denim	Three-quarter sleeved top, black	Blazer, black	Strappy heel, black	Everyday tote bag, black
1294		Casual skirt, denim	Three-quarter sleeved top, black	Blazer, black	Strappy heel, black	Small clutch, black
1295		Casual skirt, denim	Three-quarter sleeved top, black	Blazer, stone	Wedges, tan	Everyday tote bag, tan
1296		Casual skirt, denim	Three-quarter sleeved top, black	Casual jacket	Wedges, tan	Everyday tote bag, tan
1297		Casual skirt, denim	Three-quarter sleeved top, black	Casual jacket	Ballet flats, black	Everyday tote bag, black
1298		Casual skirt, denim	Three-quarter sleeved top, black	Casual jacket	Dressy sandals	Everyday tote bag, tan
1299		Casual skirt, denim	Three-quarter sleeved top, accent color		Ballet flats, black	Everyday tote bag, black
1300		Casual skirt, denim	Three-quarter sleeved top, accent color		Wedges, tan	Everyday tote bag, tan
1301		Casual skirt, denim	Three-quarter sleeved top, accent color		Strappy heel, black	Everyday tote bag, black

	TROUSER/ PANT	SKIRT/ SHORTS/ DRESS	TOP	OUTERWEAR	SHOE	BAG
1302		Casual skirt, denim	Three-quarter sleeved top, accent color		Strappy heel, black	Small clutch, black
1303		Casual skirt, denim	Three-quarter sleeved top, accent color		Wedges, tan	Everyday tote bag, tan
1304		Casual skirt, denim	Three-quarter sleeved top, accent color		Ballet flats, black	Everyday tote bag, black
1305		Casual skirt, denim	Three-quarter sleeved top, accent color		Dressy sandals	Everyday tote bag, tan
1306		Casual skirt, denim	Three-quarter sleeved top, accent color	Parka / trench coat	Ballet flats, black	Everyday tote bag, black
1307		Casual skirt, denim	Three-quarter sleeved top, accent color	Parka / trench coat	Knee-high boots, black	Everyday tote bag, black
1308		Casual skirt, denim	Three-quarter sleeved top, accent color	Blazer, black	Knee-high boots, black	Everyday tote bag, black
1309		Casual skirt, denim	Three-quarter sleeved top, accent color	Blazer, black	Wedges, tan	Everyday tote bag, tan
1310		Casual skirt, denim	Three-quarter sleeved top, accent color	Blazer, black	Strappy heel, black	Everyday tote bag, black
1311		Casual skirt, denim	Three-quarter sleeved top, accent color	Blazer, black	Strappy heel, black	Small clutch, black
1312		Casual skirt, denim	Three-quarter sleeved top, accent color	Blazer, stone	Wedges, tan	Everyday tote bag, tan
1313		Casual skirt, denim	Three-quarter sleeved top, accent color	Casual jacket	Wedges, tan	Everyday tote bag, tan
1314		Casual skirt, denim	Three-quarter sleeved top, accent color	Casual jacket	Ballet flats, black	Everyday tote bag, black
1315		Casual skirt, denim	Three-quarter sleeved top, accent color	Casual jacket	Dressy sandals	Everyday tote bag, tan
1316		Skirt, black	Basic tank, black		Round pumps, black	Everyday tote bag, black
1317		Skirt, black	Basic tank, black		Round pumps, black	Small clutch, black
1318		Skirt, black	Basic tank, black		Wedges, tan	Everyday tote bag, tan
1319		Skirt, black	Basic tank, black		Ballet flats, black	Everyday tote bag, black

TROUSER/ PANT	SKIRT/ SHORTS/ DRESS	TOP	OUTERWEAR	SHOE	BAG
	Skirt, black	Basic tank, black		Ballet flats, black	Small clutch, black
	Skirt, black	Basic tank, black		Strappy heel, black	Everyday tote bag, black
	Skirt, black	Basic tank, black		Strappy heel, black	Small clutch, black
	Skirt, black	Basic tank, black	Parka / trench coat	Knee-high boots, black	Everyday tote bag, black
	Skirt, black	Basic tank, black	Parka / trench coat	Round pumps, black	Everyday tote bag, black
	Skirt, black	Basic tank, black	Parka / trench coat	Round pumps, black	Small clutch, black
	Skirt, black	Basic tank, black	Parka / trench coat	Wedges, tan	Everyday tote bag, tan
	Skirt, black	Basic tank, black	Parka / trench coat	Ballet flats, black	Everyday tote bag, black
	Skirt, black	Basic tank, black	Parka / trench coat	Ballet flats, black	Small clutch, black
	Skirt, black	Basic tank, black	Cardigan, black	Knee-high boots, black	Everyday tote bag, black
	Skirt, black	Basic tank, black	Cardigan, black	Round pumps, black	Everyday tote bag, black
	Skirt, black	Basic tank, black	Cardigan, black	Round pumps, black	Small clutch, black
	Skirt, black	Basic tank, black	Cardigan, black	Wedges, tan	Everyday tote bag, tan
	Skirt, black	Basic tank, black	Cardigan, black	Ballet flats, black	Everyday tote bag, black
	Skirt, black	Basic tank, black	Cardigan, black	Ballet flats, black	Small clutch, black
	Skirt, black	Basic tank, black	Cardigan, black	Strappy heel, black	Everyday tote bag, black
	Skirt, black	Basic tank, black	Cardigan, black	Strappy heel, black	Small clutch, black
	Skirt, black	Basic tank, black	Blazer, black	Knee-high boots, black	Everyday tote bag, black
	Skirt, black	Basic tank, black	Blazer, black	Round pumps, black	Everyday tote bag, black
	Skirt, black	Basic tank, black	Blazer, black	Round pumps, black	Small clutch, black
	Skirt, black	Basic tank, black	Blazer, black	Wedges, tan	Everyday tote bag, tan
	Skirt, black	Basic tank, black	Blazer, black	Ballet flats, black	Everyday tote bag, black
	Skirt, black	Basic tank, black	Blazer, black	Ballet flats, black	Small clutch, black
	Skirt, black	Basic tank, black	Blazer, black	Strappy heel, black	Everyday tote bag, black
	Skirt, black	Basic tank, black	Blazer, black	Strappy heel, black	Small clutch, black
	Skirt, black	Basic tank, black	Blazer, stone	Knee-high boots, black	Everyday tote bag, black
	Skirt, black	Basic tank, black	Blazer, stone	Round pumps, black	Everyday tote bag, black

Row numbers: 1320, 1321, 1322, 1323, 1324, 1325, 1326, 1327, 1328, 1329, 1330, 1331, 1332, 1333, 1334, 1335, 1336, 1337, 1338, 1339, 1340, 1341, 1342, 1343, 1344, 1345, 1346

TROUSER/ PANT	SKIRT/ SHORTS/ DRESS	TOP	OUTERWEAR	SHOE	BAG
1347		Skirt, black	Basic tank, black	Blazer, stone	Round pumps, black	Small clutch, black
1348		Skirt, black	Basic tank, black	Blazer, stone	Wedges, tan	Everyday tote bag, tan
1349		Skirt, black	Basic tank, black	Blazer, stone	Ballet flats, black	Everyday tote bag, black
1350		Skirt, black	Basic tank, black	Blazer, stone	Ballet flats, black	Small clutch, black
1351		Skirt, black	Basic tank, black	Blazer, stone	Strappy heel, black	Everyday tote bag, black
1352		Skirt, black	Basic tank, black	Blazer, stone	Strappy heel, black	Small clutch, black
1353		Skirt, black	Basic tank, black	Casual jacket	Knee-high boots, black	Everyday tote bag, black
1354		Skirt, black	Basic tank, black	Casual jacket	Ballet flats, black	Everyday tote bag, black
1355		Skirt, black	Basic tank, black	Casual jacket	Wedges, tan	Everyday tote bag, tan
1356		Skirt, black	Basic tank, white		Round pumps, black	Everyday tote bag, black
1357		Skirt, black	Basic tank, white		Round pumps, black	Small clutch, black
1358		Skirt, black	Basic tank, white		Wedges, tan	Everyday tote bag, tan
1359		Skirt, black	Basic tank, white		Ballet flats, black	Everyday tote bag, black
1360		Skirt, black	Basic tank, white		Ballet flats, black	Small clutch, black
1361		Skirt, black	Basic tank, white		Strappy heel, black	Everyday tote bag, black
1362		Skirt, black	Basic tank, white		Strappy heel, black	Small clutch, black
1363		Skirt, black	Basic tank, white	Parka / trench coat	Knee-high boots, black	Everyday tote bag, black
1364		Skirt, black	Basic tank, white	Parka / trench coat	Round pumps, black	Everyday tote bag, black
1365		Skirt, black	Basic tank, white	Parka / trench coat	Round pumps, black	Small clutch, black
1366		Skirt, black	Basic tank, white	Parka / trench coat	Wedges, tan	Everyday tote bag, tan
1367		Skirt, black	Basic tank, white	Parka / trench coat	Ballet flats, black	Everyday tote bag, black
1368		Skirt, black	Basic tank, white	Parka / trench coat	Ballet flats, black	Small clutch, black
1369		Skirt, black	Basic tank, white	Cardigan, black	Knee-high boots, black	Everyday tote bag, black
1370		Skirt, black	Basic tank, white	Cardigan, black	Round pumps, black	Everyday tote bag, black
1371		Skirt, black	Basic tank, white	Cardigan, black	Round pumps, black	Small clutch, black
1372		Skirt, black	Basic tank, white	Cardigan, black	Wedges, tan	Everyday tote bag, tan
1373		Skirt, black	Basic tank, white	Cardigan, black	Ballet flats, black	Everyday tote bag, black

TROUSER/ PANT	SKIRT/ SHORTS/ DRESS	TOP	OUTERWEAR	SHOE	BAG
1374	Skirt, black	Basic tank, white	Cardigan, black	Ballet flats, black	Small clutch, black
1375	Skirt, black	Basic tank, white	Cardigan, black	Strappy heel, black	Everyday tote bag, black
1376	Skirt, black	Basic tank, white	Cardigan, black	Strappy heel, black	Small clutch, black
1377	Skirt, black	Basic tank, white	Blazer, black	Knee-high boots, black	Everyday tote bag, black
1378	Skirt, black	Basic tank, white	Blazer, black	Round pumps, black	Everyday tote bag, black
1379	Skirt, black	Basic tank, white	Blazer, black	Round pumps, black	Small clutch, black
1380	Skirt, black	Basic tank, white	Blazer, black	Wedges, tan	Everyday tote bag, tan
1381	Skirt, black	Basic tank, white	Blazer, black	Ballet flats, black	Everyday tote bag, black
1382	Skirt, black	Basic tank, white	Blazer, black	Ballet flats, black	Small clutch, black
1383	Skirt, black	Basic tank, white	Blazer, black	Strappy heel, black	Everyday tote bag, black
1384	Skirt, black	Basic tank, white	Blazer, black	Strappy heel, black	Small clutch, black
1385	Skirt, black	Basic tank, white	Blazer, stone	Knee-high boots, black	Everyday tote bag, black
1386	Skirt, black	Basic tank, white	Blazer, stone	Round pumps, black	Everyday tote bag, black
1387	Skirt, black	Basic tank, white	Blazer, stone	Round pumps, black	Small clutch, black
1388	Skirt, black	Basic tank, white	Blazer, stone	Wedges, tan	Everyday tote bag, tan
1389	Skirt, black	Basic tank, white	Blazer, stone	Ballet flats, black	Everyday tote bag, black
1390	Skirt, black	Basic tank, white	Blazer, stone	Ballet flats, black	Small clutch, black
1391	Skirt, black	Basic tank, white	Blazer, stone	Strappy heel, black	Everyday tote bag, black
1392	Skirt, black	Basic tank, white	Blazer, stone	Strappy heel, black	Small clutch, black
1393	Skirt, black	Basic tank, white	Casual jacket	Knee-high boots, black	Everyday tote bag, black
1394	Skirt, black	Basic tank, white	Casual jacket	Ballet flats, black	Everyday tote bag, black
1395	Skirt, black	Basic tank, white	Casual jacket	Wedges, tan	Everyday tote bag, tan
1396	Skirt, black	Blouse, accent color		Round pumps, black	Everyday tote bag, black
1397	Skirt, black	Blouse, accent color		Round pumps, black	Small clutch, black
1398	Skirt, black	Blouse, accent color		Wedges, tan	Everyday tote bag, tan
1399	Skirt, black	Blouse, accent color		Ballet flats, black	Everyday tote bag, black
1400	Skirt, black	Blouse, accent color		Ballet flats, black	Small clutch, black

#	TROUSER/ PANT	SKIRT/ SHORTS/ DRESS	TOP	OUTERWEAR	SHOE	BAG
1401		Skirt, black	Blouse, accent color		Strappy heel, black	Everyday tote bag, black
1402		Skirt, black	Blouse, accent color		Strappy heel, black	Small clutch, black
1403		Skirt, black	Blouse, accent color	Parka / trench coat	Knee-high boots, black	Everyday tote bag, black
1404		Skirt, black	Blouse, accent color	Parka / trench coat	Round pumps, black	Everyday tote bag, black
1405		Skirt, black	Blouse, accent color	Parka / trench coat	Round pumps, black	Small clutch, black
1406		Skirt, black	Blouse, accent color	Parka / trench coat	Wedges, tan	Everyday tote bag, tan
1407		Skirt, black	Blouse, accent color	Parka / trench coat	Ballet flats, black	Everyday tote bag, black
1408		Skirt, black	Blouse, accent color	Parka / trench coat	Ballet flats, black	Small clutch, black
1409		Skirt, black	Blouse, accent color	Cardigan, black	Knee-high boots, black	Everyday tote bag, black
1410		Skirt, black	Blouse, accent color	Cardigan, black	Round pumps, black	Everyday tote bag, black
1411		Skirt, black	Blouse, accent color	Cardigan, black	Round pumps, black	Small clutch, black
1412		Skirt, black	Blouse, accent color	Cardigan, black	Wedges, tan	Everyday tote bag, tan
1413		Skirt, black	Blouse, accent color	Cardigan, black	Ballet flats, black	Everyday tote bag, black
1414		Skirt, black	Blouse, accent color	Cardigan, black	Ballet flats, black	Small clutch, black
1415		Skirt, black	Blouse, accent color	Cardigan, black	Strappy heel, black	Everyday tote bag, black
1416		Skirt, black	Blouse, accent color	Cardigan, black	Strappy heel, black	Small clutch, black
1417		Skirt, black	Blouse, accent color	Blazer, black	Knee-high boots, black	Everyday tote bag, black
1418		Skirt, black	Blouse, accent color	Blazer, black	Round pumps, black	Everyday tote bag, black
1419		Skirt, black	Blouse, accent color	Blazer, black	Round pumps, black	Small clutch, black
1420		Skirt, black	Blouse, accent color	Blazer, black	Wedges, tan	Everyday tote bag, tan
1421		Skirt, black	Blouse, accent color	Blazer, black	Ballet flats, black	Everyday tote bag, black
1422		Skirt, black	Blouse, accent color	Blazer, black	Ballet flats, black	Small clutch, black
1423		Skirt, black	Blouse, accent color	Blazer, black	Strappy heel, black	Everyday tote bag, black
1424		Skirt, black	Blouse, accent color	Blazer, black	Strappy heel, black	Small clutch, black
1425		Skirt, black	Blouse, accent color	Blazer, stone	Knee-high boots, black	Everyday tote bag, black
1426		Skirt, black	Blouse, accent color	Blazer, stone	Round pumps, black	Everyday tote bag, black

	TROUSER/PANT	SKIRT/SHORTS/DRESS	TOP	OUTERWEAR	SHOE	BAG
1427		Skirt, black	Blouse, accent color	Blazer, stone	Round pumps, black	Small clutch, black
1428		Skirt, black	Blouse, accent color	Blazer, stone	Wedges, tan	Everyday tote bag, tan
1429		Skirt, black	Blouse, accent color	Blazer, stone	Ballet flats, black	Everyday tote bag, black
1430		Skirt, black	Blouse, accent color	Blazer, stone	Ballet flats, black	Small clutch, black
1431		Skirt, black	Blouse, accent color	Blazer, stone	Strappy heel, black	Everyday tote bag, black
1432		Skirt, black	Blouse, accent color	Blazer, stone	Strappy heel, black	Small clutch, black
1433		Skirt, black	Blouse, accent color	Casual jacket	Knee-high boots, black	Everyday tote bag, black
1434		Skirt, black	Blouse, accent color	Casual jacket	Ballet flats, black	Everyday tote bag, black
1435		Skirt, black	Blouse, accent color	Casual jacket	Wedges, tan	Everyday tote bag, tan
1436		Skirt, black	Second blouse, accent color		Round pumps, black	Everyday tote bag, black
1437		Skirt, black	Second blouse, accent color		Round pumps, black	Small clutch, black
1438		Skirt, black	Second blouse, accent color		Wedges, tan	Everyday tote bag, tan
1439		Skirt, black	Second blouse, accent color		Ballet flats, black	Everyday tote bag, black
1440		Skirt, black	Second blouse, accent color		Ballet flats, black	Small clutch, black
1441		Skirt, black	Second blouse, accent color		Strappy heel, black	Everyday tote bag, black
1442		Skirt, black	Second blouse, accent color		Strappy heel, black	Small clutch, black
1443		Skirt, black	Second blouse, accent color	Parka / trench coat	Knee-high boots, black	Everyday tote bag, black
1444		Skirt, black	Second blouse, accent color	Parka / trench coat	Round pumps, black	Everyday tote bag, black
1445		Skirt, black	Second blouse, accent color	Parka / trench coat	Round pumps, black	Small clutch, black
1446		Skirt, black	Second blouse, accent color	Parka / trench coat	Wedges, tan	Everyday tote bag, tan
1447		Skirt, black	Second blouse, accent color	Parka / trench coat	Ballet flats, black	Everyday tote bag, black
1448		Skirt, black	Second blouse, accent color	Parka / trench coat	Ballet flats, black	Small clutch, black
1449		Skirt, black	Second blouse, accent color	Cardigan, black	Knee-high boots, black	Everyday tote bag, black
1450		Skirt, black	Second blouse, accent color	Cardigan, black	Round pumps, black	Everyday tote bag, black
1451		Skirt, black	Second blouse, accent color	Cardigan, black	Round pumps, black	Small clutch, black
1452		Skirt, black	Second blouse, accent color	Cardigan, black	Wedges, tan	Everyday tote bag, tan
1453		Skirt, black	Second blouse, accent color	Cardigan, black	Ballet flats, black	Everyday tote bag, black

	TROUSER/ PANT	SKIRT/ SHORTS/ DRESS	TOP	OUTERWEAR	SHOE	BAG
1454		Skirt, black	Second blouse, accent color	Cardigan, black	Ballet flats, black	Small clutch, black
1455		Skirt, black	Second blouse, accent color	Cardigan, black	Strappy heel, black	Everyday tote bag, black
1456		Skirt, black	Second blouse, accent color	Cardigan, black	Strappy heel, black	Small clutch, black
1457		Skirt, black	Second blouse, accent color	Blazer, black	Knee-high boots, black	Everyday tote bag, black
1458		Skirt, black	Second blouse, accent color	Blazer, black	Round pumps, black	Everyday tote bag, black
1459		Skirt, black	Second blouse, accent color	Blazer, black	Round pumps, black	Small clutch, black
1460		Skirt, black	Second blouse, accent color	Blazer, black	Wedges, tan	Everyday tote bag, tan
1461		Skirt, black	Second blouse, accent color	Blazer, black	Ballet flats, black	Everyday tote bag, black
1462		Skirt, black	Second blouse, accent color	Blazer, black	Ballet flats, black	Small clutch, black
1463		Skirt, black	Second blouse, accent color	Blazer, black	Strappy heel, black	Everyday tote bag, black
1464		Skirt, black	Second blouse, accent color	Blazer, black	Strappy heel, black	Small clutch, black
1465		Skirt, black	Second blouse, accent color	Blazer, stone	Knee-high boots, black	Everyday tote bag, black
1466		Skirt, black	Second blouse, accent color	Blazer, stone	Round pumps, black	Everyday tote bag, black
1467		Skirt, black	Second blouse, accent color	Blazer, stone	Round pumps, black	Small clutch, black
1468		Skirt, black	Second blouse, accent color	Blazer, stone	Wedges, tan	Everyday tote bag, tan
1469		Skirt, black	Second blouse, accent color	Blazer, stone	Ballet flats, black	Everyday tote bag, black
1470		Skirt, black	Second blouse, accent color	Blazer, stone	Ballet flats, black	Small clutch, black
1471		Skirt, black	Second blouse, accent color	Blazer, stone	Strappy heel, black	Everyday tote bag, black
1472		Skirt, black	Second blouse, accent color	Blazer, stone	Strappy heel, black	Small clutch, black
1473		Skirt, black	Second blouse, accent color	Casual jacket	Knee-high boots, black	Everyday tote bag, black
1474		Skirt, black	Second blouse, accent color	Casual jacket	Ballet flats, black	Everyday tote bag, black
1475		Skirt, black	Second blouse, accent color	Casual jacket	Wedges, tan	Everyday tote bag, tan
1476		Skirt, black	Three-quarter sleeved top, black		Round pumps, black	Everyday tote bag, black
1477		Skirt, black	Three-quarter sleeved top, black		Round pumps, black	Small clutch, black
1478		Skirt, black	Three-quarter sleeved top, black		Wedges, tan	Everyday tote bag, tan

211

TROUSER/ PANT	SKIRT/ SHORTS/ DRESS	TOP	OUTERWEAR	SHOE	BAG
1479		Skirt, black	Three-quarter sleeved top, black		Ballet flats, black	Everyday tote bag, black
1480		Skirt, black	Three-quarter sleeved top, black		Ballet flats, black	Small clutch, black
1481		Skirt, black	Three-quarter sleeved top, black		Strappy heel, black	Everyday tote bag, black
1482		Skirt, black	Three-quarter sleeved top, black		Strappy heel, black	Small clutch, black
1483		Skirt, black	Three-quarter sleeved top, black	Parka / trench coat	Knee-high boots, black	Everyday tote bag, black
1484		Skirt, black	Three-quarter sleeved top, black	Parka / trench coat	Round pumps, black	Everyday tote bag, black
1485		Skirt, black	Three-quarter sleeved top, black	Parka / trench coat	Round pumps, black	Small clutch, black
1486		Skirt, black	Three-quarter sleeved top, black	Parka / trench coat	Wedges, tan	Everyday tote bag, tan
1487		Skirt, black	Three-quarter sleeved top, black	Parka / trench coat	Ballet flats, black	Everyday tote bag, black
1488		Skirt, black	Three-quarter sleeved top, black	Parka / trench coat	Ballet flats, black	Small clutch, black
1489		Skirt, black	Three-quarter sleeved top, black	Cardigan, black	Knee-high boots, black	Everyday tote bag, black
1490		Skirt, black	Three-quarter sleeved top, black	Cardigan, black	Round pumps, black	Everyday tote bag, black
1491		Skirt, black	Three-quarter sleeved top, black	Cardigan, black	Round pumps, black	Small clutch, black
1492		Skirt, black	Three-quarter sleeved top, black	Cardigan, black	Wedges, tan	Everyday tote bag, tan
1493		Skirt, black	Three-quarter sleeved top, black	Cardigan, black	Ballet flats, black	Everyday tote bag, black

TROUSER/PANT	SKIRT/SHORTS/DRESS	TOP	OUTERWEAR	SHOE	BAG
1494	Skirt, black	Three-quarter sleeved top, black	Cardigan, black	Ballet flats, black	Small clutch, black
1495	Skirt, black	Three-quarter sleeved top, black	Cardigan, black	Strappy heel, black	Everyday tote bag, black
1496	Skirt, black	Three-quarter sleeved top, black	Cardigan, black	Strappy heel, black	Small clutch, black
1497	Skirt, black	Three-quarter sleeved top, black	Blazer, black	Knee-high boots, black	Everyday tote bag, black
1498	Skirt, black	Three-quarter sleeved top, black	Blazer, black	Round pumps, black	Everyday tote bag, black
1499	Skirt, black	Three-quarter sleeved top, black	Blazer, black	Round pumps, black	Small clutch, black
1500	Skirt, black	Three-quarter sleeved top, black	Blazer, black	Wedges, tan	Everyday tote bag, tan
1501	Skirt, black	Three-quarter sleeved top, black	Blazer, black	Ballet flats, black	Everyday tote bag, black
1502	Skirt, black	Three-quarter sleeved top, black	Blazer, black	Ballet flats, black	Small clutch, black
1503	Skirt, black	Three-quarter sleeved top, black	Blazer, black	Strappy heel, black	Everyday tote bag, black
1504	Skirt, black	Three-quarter sleeved top, black	Blazer, black	Strappy heel, black	Small clutch, black
1505	Skirt, black	Three-quarter sleeved top, black	Blazer, stone	Knee-high boots, black	Everyday tote bag, black
1506	Skirt, black	Three-quarter sleeved top, black	Blazer, stone	Round pumps, black	Everyday tote bag, black
1507	Skirt, black	Three-quarter sleeved top, black	Blazer, stone	Round pumps, black	Small clutch, black
1508	Skirt, black	Three-quarter sleeved top, black	Blazer, stone	Wedges, tan	Everyday tote bag, tan
1509	Skirt, black	Three-quarter sleeved top, black	Blazer, stone	Ballet flats, black	Everyday tote bag, black

	TROUSER/PANT	SKIRT/SHORTS/DRESS	TOP	OUTERWEAR	SHOE	BAG
1510		Skirt, black	Three-quarter sleeved top, black	Blazer, stone	Ballet flats, black	Small clutch, black
1511		Skirt, black	Three-quarter sleeved top, black	Blazer, stone	Strappy heel, black	Everyday tote bag, black
1512		Skirt, black	Three-quarter sleeved top, black	Blazer, stone	Strappy heel, black	Small clutch, black
1513		Skirt, black	Three-quarter sleeved top, black	Casual jacket	Knee-high boots, black	Everyday tote bag, black
1514		Skirt, black	Three-quarter sleeved top, black	Casual jacket	Ballet flats, black	Everyday tote bag, black
1515		Skirt, black	Three-quarter sleeved top, black	Casual jacket	Wedges, tan	Everyday tote bag, tan
1516		Skirt, black	Three-quarter sleeved top, accent color		Round pumps, black	Everyday tote bag, black
1517		Skirt, black	Three-quarter sleeved top, accent color		Round pumps, black	Small clutch, black
1518		Skirt, black	Three-quarter sleeved top, accent color		Wedges, tan	Everyday tote bag, tan
1519		Skirt, black	Three-quarter sleeved top, accent color		Ballet flats, black	Everyday tote bag, black
1520		Skirt, black	Three-quarter sleeved top, accent color		Ballet flats, black	Small clutch, black
1521		Skirt, black	Three-quarter sleeved top, accent color		Strappy heel, black	Everyday tote bag, black
1522		Skirt, black	Three-quarter sleeved top, accent color		Strappy heel, black	Small clutch, black
1523		Skirt, black	Three-quarter sleeved top, accent color	Parka / trench coat	Knee-high boots, black	Everyday tote bag, black
1524		Skirt, black	Three-quarter sleeved top, accent color	Parka / trench coat	Round pumps, black	Everyday tote bag, black

	TROUSER/PANT	SKIRT/SHORTS/DRESS	TOP	OUTERWEAR	SHOE	BAG
1525		Skirt, black	Three-quarter sleeved top, accent color	Parka / trench coat	Round pumps, black	Small clutch, black
1526		Skirt, black	Three-quarter sleeved top, accent color	Parka / trench coat	Wedges, tan	Everyday tote bag, tan
1527		Skirt, black	Three-quarter sleeved top, accent color	Parka / trench coat	Ballet flats, black	Everyday tote bag, black
1528		Skirt, black	Three-quarter sleeved top, accent color	Parka / trench coat	Ballet flats, black	Small clutch, black
1529		Skirt, black	Three-quarter sleeved top, accent color	Cardigan, black	Knee-high boots, black	Everyday tote bag, black
1530		Skirt, black	Three-quarter sleeved top, accent color	Cardigan, black	Round pumps, black	Everyday tote bag, black
1531		Skirt, black	Three-quarter sleeved top, accent color	Cardigan, black	Round pumps, black	Small clutch, black
1532		Skirt, black	Three-quarter sleeved top, accent color	Cardigan, black	Wedges, tan	Everyday tote bag, tan
1533		Skirt, black	Three-quarter sleeved top, accent color	Cardigan, black	Ballet flats, black	Everyday tote bag, black
1534		Skirt, black	Three-quarter sleeved top, accent color	Cardigan, black	Ballet flats, black	Small clutch, black
1535		Skirt, black	Three-quarter sleeved top, accent color	Cardigan, black	Strappy heel, black	Everyday tote bag, black
1536		Skirt, black	Three-quarter sleeved top, accent color	Cardigan, black	Strappy heel, black	Small clutch, black
1537		Skirt, black	Three-quarter sleeved top, accent color	Blazer, black	Knee-high boots, black	Everyday tote bag, black
1538		Skirt, black	Three-quarter sleeved top, accent color	Blazer, black	Round pumps, black	Everyday tote bag, black
1539		Skirt, black	Three-quarter sleeved top, accent color	Blazer, black	Round pumps, black	Small clutch, black

	TROUSER/PANT	SKIRT/SHORTS/DRESS	TOP	OUTERWEAR	SHOE	BAG
1540		Skirt, black	Three-quarter sleeved top, accent color	Blazer, black	Wedges, tan	Everyday tote bag, tan
1541		Skirt, black	Three-quarter sleeved top, accent color	Blazer, black	Ballet flats, black	Everyday tote bag, black
1542		Skirt, black	Three-quarter sleeved top, accent color	Blazer, black	Ballet flats, black	Small clutch, black
1543		Skirt, black	Three-quarter sleeved top, accent color	Blazer, black	Strappy heel, black	Everyday tote bag, black
1544		Skirt, black	Three-quarter sleeved top, accent color	Blazer, black	Strappy heel, black	Small clutch, black
1545		Skirt, black	Three-quarter sleeved top, accent color	Blazer, stone	Knee-high boots, black	Everyday tote bag, black
1546		Skirt, black	Three-quarter sleeved top, accent color	Blazer, stone	Round pumps, black	Everyday tote bag, black
1547		Skirt, black	Three-quarter sleeved top, accent color	Blazer, stone	Round pumps, black	Small clutch, black
1548		Skirt, black	Three-quarter sleeved top, accent color	Blazer, stone	Wedges, tan	Everyday tote bag, tan
1549		Skirt, black	Three-quarter sleeved top, accent color	Blazer, stone	Ballet flats, black	Everyday tote bag, black
1550		Skirt, black	Three-quarter sleeved top, accent color	Blazer, stone	Ballet flats, black	Small clutch, black
1551		Skirt, black	Three-quarter sleeved top, accent color	Blazer, stone	Strappy heel, black	Everyday tote bag, black
1552		Skirt, black	Three-quarter sleeved top, accent color	Blazer, stone	Strappy heel, black	Small clutch, black
1553		Skirt, black	Three-quarter sleeved top, accent color	Casual jacket	Knee-high boots, black	Everyday tote bag, black
1554		Skirt, black	Three-quarter sleeved top, accent color	Casual jacket	Ballet flats, black	Everyday tote bag, black

	TROUSER/PANT	SKIRT/SHORTS/DRESS	TOP	OUTERWEAR	SHOE	BAG
1555		Skirt, black	Three-quarter sleeved top, accent color	Casual jacket	Wedges, tan	Everyday tote bag, tan
1556		Tailored shorts	Basic tank, black		Round pumps, black	Everyday tote bag, black
1557		Tailored shorts	Basic tank, black		Round pumps, black	Small clutch, black
1558		Tailored shorts	Basic tank, black		Strappy heel, black	Everyday tote bag, black
1559		Tailored shorts	Basic tank, black		Strappy heel, black	Small clutch, black
1560		Tailored shorts	Basic tank, black		Wedges, tan	Everyday tote bag, tan
1561		Tailored shorts	Basic tank, black		Ballet flats, black	Everyday tote bag, black
1562		Tailored shorts	Basic tank, black		Dressy sandals	Everyday tote bag, tan
1563		Tailored shorts	Basic tank, black	Cardigan, black	Round pumps, black	Everyday tote bag, black
1564		Tailored shorts	Basic tank, black	Cardigan, black	Round pumps, black	Small clutch, black
1565		Tailored shorts	Basic tank, black	Cardigan, black	Strappy heel, black	Everyday tote bag, black
1566		Tailored shorts	Basic tank, black	Cardigan, black	Strappy heel, black	Small clutch, black
1567		Tailored shorts	Basic tank, black	Cardigan, black	Wedges, tan	Everyday tote bag, tan
1568		Tailored shorts	Basic tank, black	Cardigan, black	Ballet flats, black	Everyday tote bag, black
1569		Tailored shorts	Basic tank, black	Cardigan, black	Dressy sandals	Everyday tote bag, tan
1570		Tailored shorts	Basic tank, black	Blazer, black	Round pumps, black	Everyday tote bag, black
1571		Tailored shorts	Basic tank, black	Blazer, black	Round pumps, black	Small clutch, black
1572		Tailored shorts	Basic tank, black	Blazer, black	Strappy heel, black	Everyday tote bag, black
1573		Tailored shorts	Basic tank, black	Blazer, black	Strappy heel, black	Small clutch, black
1574		Tailored shorts	Basic tank, black	Blazer, black	Wedges, tan	Everyday tote bag, tan
1575		Tailored shorts	Basic tank, black	Blazer, black	Ballet flats, black	Everyday tote bag, black
1576		Tailored shorts	Basic tank, black	Blazer, stone	Round pumps, black	Everyday tote bag, black
1577		Tailored shorts	Basic tank, black	Blazer, stone	Round pumps, black	Small clutch, black
1578		Tailored shorts	Basic tank, black	Blazer, stone	Strappy heel, black	Everyday tote bag, black
1579		Tailored shorts	Basic tank, black	Blazer, stone	Strappy heel, black	Small clutch, black

	SKIRT/SHORTS/DRESS	TOP	OUTERWEAR	SHOE	BAG
1580	Tailored shorts	Basic tank, black	Blazer, stone	Wedges, tan	Everyday tote bag, tan
1581	Tailored shorts	Basic tank, black	Blazer, stone	Ballet flats, black	Everyday tote bag, black
1582	Tailored shorts	Basic tank, black	Casual jacket	Wedges, tan	Everyday tote bag, tan
1583	Tailored shorts	Basic tank, black	Casual jacket	Ballet flats, black	Everyday tote bag, black
1584	Tailored shorts	Basic tank, black	Casual jacket	Dressy sandals	Everyday tote bag, tan
1585	Tailored shorts	Basic tank, white		Round pumps, black	Everyday tote bag, black
1586	Tailored shorts	Basic tank, white		Round pumps, black	Small clutch, black
1587	Tailored shorts	Basic tank, white		Strappy heel, black	Everyday tote bag, black
1588	Tailored shorts	Basic tank, white		Strappy heel, black	Small clutch, black
1589	Tailored shorts	Basic tank, white		Wedges, tan	Everyday tote bag, tan
1590	Tailored shorts	Basic tank, white		Ballet flats, black	Everyday tote bag, black
1591	Tailored shorts	Basic tank, white		Dressy sandals	Everyday tote bag, tan
1592	Tailored shorts	Basic tank, white	Cardigan, black	Round pumps, black	Everyday tote bag, black
1593	Tailored shorts	Basic tank, white	Cardigan, black	Round pumps, black	Small clutch, black
1594	Tailored shorts	Basic tank, white	Cardigan, black	Strappy heel, black	Everyday tote bag, black
1595	Tailored shorts	Basic tank, white	Cardigan, black	Strappy heel, black	Small clutch, black
1596	Tailored shorts	Basic tank, white	Cardigan, black	Wedges, tan	Everyday tote bag, tan
1597	Tailored shorts	Basic tank, white	Cardigan, black	Ballet flats, black	Everyday tote bag, black
1598	Tailored shorts	Basic tank, white	Cardigan, black	Dressy sandals	Everyday tote bag, tan
1599	Tailored shorts	Basic tank, white	Blazer, black	Round pumps, black	Everyday tote bag, black
1600	Tailored shorts	Basic tank, white	Blazer, black	Round pumps, black	Small clutch, black
1601	Tailored shorts	Basic tank, white	Blazer, black	Strappy heel, black	Everyday tote bag, black
1602	Tailored shorts	Basic tank, white	Blazer, black	Strappy heel, black	Small clutch, black
1603	Tailored shorts	Basic tank, white	Blazer, black	Wedges, tan	Everyday tote bag, tan
1604	Tailored shorts	Basic tank, white	Blazer, black	Ballet flats, black	Everyday tote bag, black
1605	Tailored shorts	Basic tank, white	Blazer, stone	Round pumps, black	Everyday tote bag, black

TROUSER/ PANT	SKIRT/ SHORTS/ DRESS	TOP	OUTERWEAR	SHOE	BAG
1606	Tailored shorts	Basic tank, white	Blazer, stone	Round pumps, black	Small clutch, black
1607	Tailored shorts	Basic tank, white	Blazer, stone	Strappy heel, black	Everyday tote bag, black
1608	Tailored shorts	Basic tank, white	Blazer, stone	Strappy heel, black	Small clutch, black
1609	Tailored shorts	Basic tank, white	Blazer, stone	Wedges, tan	Everyday tote bag, tan
1610	Tailored shorts	Basic tank, white	Blazer, stone	Ballet flats, black	Everyday tote bag, black
1611	Tailored shorts	Basic tank, white	Casual jacket	Wedges, tan	Everyday tote bag, tan
1612	Tailored shorts	Basic tank, white	Casual jacket	Ballet flats, black	Everyday tote bag, black
1613	Tailored shorts	Basic tank, white	Casual jacket	Dressy sandals	Everyday tote bag, tan
1614	Tailored shorts	Blouse, accent color		Round pumps, black	Everyday tote bag, black
1615	Tailored shorts	Blouse, accent color		Round pumps, black	Small clutch, black
1616	Tailored shorts	Blouse, accent color		Strappy heel, black	Everyday tote bag, black
1617	Tailored shorts	Blouse, accent color		Strappy heel, black	Small clutch, black
1618	Tailored shorts	Blouse, accent color		Wedges, tan	Everyday tote bag, tan
1619	Tailored shorts	Blouse, accent color		Ballet flats, black	Everyday tote bag, black
1620	Tailored shorts	Blouse, accent color		Dressy sandals	Everyday tote bag, tan
1621	Tailored shorts	Blouse, accent color	Cardigan, black	Round pumps, black	Everyday tote bag, black
1622	Tailored shorts	Blouse, accent color	Cardigan, black	Round pumps, black	Small clutch, black
1623	Tailored shorts	Blouse, accent color	Cardigan, black	Strappy heel, black	Everyday tote bag, black
1624	Tailored shorts	Blouse, accent color	Cardigan, black	Strappy heel, black	Small clutch, black
1625	Tailored shorts	Blouse, accent color	Cardigan, black	Wedges, tan	Everyday tote bag, tan
1626	Tailored shorts	Blouse, accent color	Cardigan, black	Ballet flats, black	Everyday tote bag, black
1627	Tailored shorts	Blouse, accent color	Cardigan, black	Dressy sandals	Everyday tote bag, tan
1628	Tailored shorts	Blouse, accent color	Blazer, black	Round pumps, black	Everyday tote bag, black
1629	Tailored shorts	Blouse, accent color	Blazer, black	Round pumps, black	Small clutch, black
1630	Tailored shorts	Blouse, accent color	Blazer, black	Strappy heel, black	Everyday tote bag, black
1631	Tailored shorts	Blouse, accent color	Blazer, black	Strappy heel, black	Small clutch, black

	TROUSER/ PANT	SKIRT/ SHORTS/ DRESS	TOP	OUTERWEAR	SHOE	BAG
1632		Tailored shorts	Blouse, accent color	Blazer, black	Wedges, tan	Everyday tote bag, tan
1633		Tailored shorts	Blouse, accent color	Blazer, black	Ballet flats, black	Everyday tote bag, black
1634		Tailored shorts	Blouse, accent color	Blazer, stone	Round pumps, black	Everyday tote bag, black
1635		Tailored shorts	Blouse, accent color	Blazer, stone	Round pumps, black	Small clutch, black
1636		Tailored shorts	Blouse, accent color	Blazer, stone	Strappy heel, black	Everyday tote bag, black
1637		Tailored shorts	Blouse, accent color	Blazer, stone	Strappy heel, black	Small clutch, black
1638		Tailored shorts	Blouse, accent color	Blazer, stone	Wedges, tan	Everyday tote bag, tan
1639		Tailored shorts	Blouse, accent color	Blazer, stone	Ballet flats, black	Everyday tote bag, black
1640		Tailored shorts	Blouse, accent color	Casual jacket	Wedges, tan	Everyday tote bag, tan
1641		Tailored shorts	Blouse, accent color	Casual jacket	Ballet flats, black	Everyday tote bag, black
1642		Tailored shorts	Blouse, accent color	Casual jacket	Dressy sandals	Everyday tote bag, tan
1643		Tailored shorts	Second blouse, accent color		Round pumps, black	Everyday tote bag, black
1644		Tailored shorts	Second blouse, accent color		Round pumps, black	Small clutch, black
1645		Tailored shorts	Second blouse, accent color		Strappy heel, black	Everyday tote bag, black
1646		Tailored shorts	Second blouse, accent color		Strappy heel, black	Small clutch, black
1647		Tailored shorts	Second blouse, accent color		Wedges, tan	Everyday tote bag, tan
1648		Tailored shorts	Second blouse, accent color		Ballet flats, black	Everyday tote bag, black
1649		Tailored shorts	Second blouse, accent color		Dressy sandals	Everyday tote bag, tan
1650		Tailored shorts	Second blouse, accent color	Cardigan, black	Round pumps, black	Everyday tote bag, black
1651		Tailored shorts	Second blouse, accent color	Cardigan, black	Round pumps, black	Small clutch, black
1652		Tailored shorts	Second blouse, accent color	Cardigan, black	Strappy heel, black	Everyday tote bag, black
1653		Tailored shorts	Second blouse, accent color	Cardigan, black	Strappy heel, black	Small clutch, black
1654		Tailored shorts	Second blouse, accent color	Cardigan, black	Wedges, tan	Everyday tote bag, tan
1655		Tailored shorts	Second blouse, accent color	Cardigan, black	Ballet flats, black	Everyday tote bag, black
1656		Tailored shorts	Second blouse, accent color	Cardigan, black	Dressy sandals	Everyday tote bag, tan
1657		Tailored shorts	Second blouse, accent color	Blazer, black	Round pumps, black	Everyday tote bag, black
1658		Tailored shorts	Second blouse, accent color	Blazer, black	Round pumps, black	Small clutch, black

TROUSER/PANT	SKIRT/SHORTS/DRESS	TOP	OUTERWEAR	SHOE	BAG
1659	Tailored shorts	Second blouse, accent color	Blazer, black	Strappy heel, black	Everyday tote bag, black
1660	Tailored shorts	Second blouse, accent color	Blazer, black	Strappy heel, black	Small clutch, black
1661	Tailored shorts	Second blouse, accent color	Blazer, black	Wedges, tan	Everyday tote bag, tan
1662	Tailored shorts	Second blouse, accent color	Blazer, black	Ballet flats, black	Everyday tote bag, black
1663	Tailored shorts	Second blouse, accent color	Blazer, stone	Round pumps, black	Everyday tote bag, black
1664	Tailored shorts	Second blouse, accent color	Blazer, stone	Round pumps, black	Small clutch, black
1665	Tailored shorts	Second blouse, accent color	Blazer, stone	Strappy heel, black	Everyday tote bag, black
1666	Tailored shorts	Second blouse, accent color	Blazer, stone	Strappy heel, black	Small clutch, black
1667	Tailored shorts	Second blouse, accent color	Blazer, stone	Wedges, tan	Everyday tote bag, tan
1668	Tailored shorts	Second blouse, accent color	Blazer, stone	Ballet flats, black	Everyday tote bag, black
1669	Tailored shorts	Second blouse, accent color	Casual jacket	Wedges, tan	Everyday tote bag, tan
1670	Tailored shorts	Second blouse, accent color	Casual jacket	Ballet flats, black	Everyday tote bag, black
1671	Tailored shorts	Second blouse, accent color	Casual jacket	Dressy sandals	Everyday tote bag, tan
1672	Tailored shorts	Three-quarter sleeved top, black		Round pumps, black	Everyday tote bag, black
1673	Tailored shorts	Three-quarter sleeved top, black		Round pumps, black	Small clutch, black
1674	Tailored shorts	Three-quarter sleeved top, black		Strappy heel, black	Everyday tote bag, black
1675	Tailored shorts	Three-quarter sleeved top, black		Strappy heel, black	Small clutch, black
1676	Tailored shorts	Three-quarter sleeved top, black		Wedges, tan	Everyday tote bag, tan
1677	Tailored shorts	Three-quarter sleeved top, black		Ballet flats, black	Everyday tote bag, black
1678	Tailored shorts	Three-quarter sleeved top, black		Dressy sandals	Everyday tote bag, tan
1679	Tailored shorts	Three-quarter sleeved top, black	Cardigan, black	Round pumps, black	Everyday tote bag, black

	TROUSER/PANT	SKIRT/SHORTS/DRESS	TOP	OUTERWEAR	SHOE	BAG
1680		Tailored shorts	Three-quarter sleeved top, black	Cardigan, black	Round pumps, black	Small clutch, black
1681		Tailored shorts	Three-quarter sleeved top, black	Cardigan, black	Strappy heel, black	Everyday tote bag, black
1682		Tailored shorts	Three-quarter sleeved top, black	Cardigan, black	Strappy heel, black	Small clutch, black
1683		Tailored shorts	Three-quarter sleeved top, black	Cardigan, black	Wedges, tan	Everyday tote bag, tan
1684		Tailored shorts	Three-quarter sleeved top, black	Cardigan, black	Ballet flats, black	Everyday tote bag, black
1685		Tailored shorts	Three-quarter sleeved top, black	Cardigan, black	Dressy sandals	Everyday tote bag, tan
1686		Tailored shorts	Three-quarter sleeved top, black	Blazer, black	Round pumps, black	Everyday tote bag, black
1687		Tailored shorts	Three-quarter sleeved top, black	Blazer, black	Round pumps, black	Small clutch, black
1688		Tailored shorts	Three-quarter sleeved top, black	Blazer, black	Strappy heel, black	Everyday tote bag, black
1689		Tailored shorts	Three-quarter sleeved top, black	Blazer, black	Strappy heel, black	Small clutch, black
1690		Tailored shorts	Three-quarter sleeved top, black	Blazer, black	Wedges, tan	Everyday tote bag, tan
1691		Tailored shorts	Three-quarter sleeved top, black	Blazer, black	Ballet flats, black	Everyday tote bag, black
1692		Tailored shorts	Three-quarter sleeved top, black	Blazer, stone	Round pumps, black	Everyday tote bag, black
1693		Tailored shorts	Three-quarter sleeved top, black	Blazer, stone	Round pumps, black	Small clutch, black
1694		Tailored shorts	Three-quarter sleeved top, black	Blazer, stone	Strappy heel, black	Everyday tote bag, black

	TROUSER/ PANT	SKIRT/ SHORTS/ DRESS	TOP	OUTERWEAR	SHOE	BAG
1695		Tailored shorts	Three-quarter sleeved top, black	Blazer, stone	Strappy heel, black	Small clutch, black
1696		Tailored shorts	Three-quarter sleeved top, black	Blazer, stone	Wedges, tan	Everyday tote bag, tan
1697		Tailored shorts	Three-quarter sleeved top, black	Blazer, stone	Ballet flats, black	Everyday tote bag, black
1698		Tailored shorts	Three-quarter sleeved top, black	Casual jacket	Wedges, tan	Everyday tote bag, tan
1699		Tailored shorts	Three-quarter sleeved top, black	Casual jacket	Ballet flats, black	Everyday tote bag, black
1700		Tailored shorts	Three-quarter sleeved top, black	Casual jacket	Dressy sandals	Everyday tote bag, tan
1701		Tailored shorts	Three-quarter sleeved top, accent color		Round pumps, black	Everyday tote bag, black
1702		Tailored shorts	Three-quarter sleeved top, accent color		Round pumps, black	Small clutch, black
1703		Tailored shorts	Three-quarter sleeved top, accent color		Strappy heel, black	Everyday tote bag, black
1704		Tailored shorts	Three-quarter sleeved top, accent color		Strappy heel, black	Small clutch, black
1705		Tailored shorts	Three-quarter sleeved top, accent color		Wedges, tan	Everyday tote bag, tan
1706		Tailored shorts	Three-quarter sleeved top, accent color		Ballet flats, black	Everyday tote bag, black
1707		Tailored shorts	Three-quarter sleeved top, accent color		Dressy sandals	Everyday tote bag, tan
1708		Tailored shorts	Three-quarter sleeved top, accent color	Cardigan, black	Round pumps, black	Everyday tote bag, black
1709		Tailored shorts	Three-quarter sleeved top, accent color	Cardigan, black	Round pumps, black	Small clutch, black

	TROUSER/ PANT	SKIRT/ SHORTS/ DRESS	TOP	OUTERWEAR	SHOE	BAG
1710		Tailored shorts	Three-quarter sleeved top, accent color	Cardigan, black	Strappy heel, black	Everyday tote bag, black
1711		Tailored shorts	Three-quarter sleeved top, accent color	Cardigan, black	Strappy heel, black	Small clutch, black
1712		Tailored shorts	Three-quarter sleeved top, accent color	Cardigan, black	Wedges, tan	Everyday tote bag, tan
1713		Tailored shorts	Three-quarter sleeved top, accent color	Cardigan, black	Ballet flats, black	Everyday tote bag, black
1714		Tailored shorts	Three-quarter sleeved top, accent color	Cardigan, black	Dressy sandals	Everyday tote bag, tan
1715		Tailored shorts	Three-quarter sleeved top, accent color	Blazer, black	Round pumps, black	Everyday tote bag, black
1716		Tailored shorts	Three-quarter sleeved top, accent color	Blazer, black	Round pumps, black	Small clutch, black
1717		Tailored shorts	Three-quarter sleeved top, accent color	Blazer, black	Strappy heel, black	Everyday tote bag, black
1718		Tailored shorts	Three-quarter sleeved top, accent color	Blazer, black	Strappy heel, black	Small clutch, black
1719		Tailored shorts	Three-quarter sleeved top, accent color	Blazer, black	Wedges, tan	Everyday tote bag, tan
1720		Tailored shorts	Three-quarter sleeved top, accent color	Blazer, black	Ballet flats, black	Everyday tote bag, black
1721		Tailored shorts	Three-quarter sleeved top, accent color	Blazer, stone	Round pumps, black	Everyday tote bag, black
1722		Tailored shorts	Three-quarter sleeved top, accent color	Blazer, stone	Round pumps, black	Small clutch, black
1723		Tailored shorts	Three-quarter sleeved top, accent color	Blazer, stone	Strappy heel, black	Everyday tote bag, black
1724		Tailored shorts	Three-quarter sleeved top, accent color	Blazer, stone	Strappy heel, black	Small clutch, black

	TROUSER/ PANT	SKIRT/ SHORTS/ DRESS	TOP	OUTERWEAR	SHOE	BAG
1725		Tailored shorts	Three-quarter sleeved top, accent color	Blazer, stone	Wedges, tan	Everyday tote bag, tan
1726		Tailored shorts	Three-quarter sleeved top, accent color	Blazer, stone	Ballet flats, black	Everyday tote bag, black
1727		Tailored shorts	Three-quarter sleeved top, accent color	Casual jacket	Wedges, tan	Everyday tote bag, tan
1728		Tailored shorts	Three-quarter sleeved top, accent color	Casual jacket	Ballet flats, black	Everyday tote bag, black
1729		Tailored shorts	Three-quarter sleeved top, accent color	Casual jacket	Dressy sandals	Everyday tote bag, tan
1730		Casual day dress			Wedges, tan	Everyday tote bag, tan
1731		Casual day dress			Strappy heel, black	Everyday tote bag, black
1732		Casual day dress			Strappy heel, black	Small clutch, black
1733		Casual day dress			Ballet flats, black	Everyday tote bag, black
1734		Casual day dress			Ballet flats, black	Small clutch, black
1735		Casual day dress			Dressy sandals	Everyday tote bag, tan
1736		Casual day dress			Dressy sandals	Small clutch, black
1737		Casual day dress		Cardigan, black	Strappy heel, black	Everyday tote bag, black
1738		Casual day dress		Cardigan, black	Strappy heel, black	Small clutch, black
1739		Casual day dress		Cardigan, black	Ballet flats, black	Everyday tote bag, black

TROUSER/PANT	SKIRT/SHORTS/DRESS	TOP	OUTERWEAR	SHOE	BAG
1740	Casual day dress		Cardigan, black	Ballet flats, black	Everyday tote bag, tan
1741	Casual day dress		Cardigan, black	Ballet flats, black	Small clutch, black
1742	Casual day dress		Cardigan, black	Dressy sandals	Small clutch, black
1743	Casual day dress		Blazer, black	Wedges, tan	Everyday tote bag, tan
1744	Casual day dress		Blazer, black	Strappy heel, black	Everyday tote bag, black
1745	Casual day dress		Blazer, black	Strappy heel, black	Small clutch, black
1746	Casual day dress		Blazer, black	Strappy heel, black	Everyday tote bag, tan
1747	Casual day dress		Blazer, black	Ballet flats, black	Everyday tote bag, black
1748	Casual day dress		Blazer, black	Ballet flats, black	Small clutch, black
1749	Casual day dress		Blazer, black	Round pumps, black	Everyday tote bag, black
1750	Casual day dress		Blazer, black	Round pumps, black	Small clutch, black
1751	Casual day dress		Blazer, stone	Wedges, tan	Everyday tote bag, tan
1752	Casual day dress		Blazer, stone	Strappy heel, black	Everyday tote bag, black
1753	Casual day dress		Blazer, stone	Strappy heel, black	Small clutch, black
1754	Casual day dress		Blazer, stone	Strappy heel, black	Everyday tote bag, tan

	TROUSER/PANT	SKIRT/SHORTS/DRESS	TOP	OUTERWEAR	SHOE	BAG
1755		Casual day dress		Blazer, stone	Ballet flats, black	Everyday tote bag, black
1756		Casual day dress		Blazer, stone	Ballet flats, black	Small clutch, black
1757		Casual day dress		Blazer, stone	Round pumps, black	Everyday tote bag, black
1758		Casual day dress		Blazer, stone	Round pumps, black	Small clutch, black
1759		Casual day dress		Blazer, stone	Dressy sandals	Everyday tote bag, tan
1760		Casual day dress		Casual jacket	Wedges, tan	Everyday tote bag, tan
1761		Casual day dress		Casual jacket	Ballet flats, black	Everyday tote bag, black
1762		Casual day dress		Casual jacket	Dressy sandals	Everyday tote bag, tan
1763		Casual day dress		Parka / trench coat	Knee-high boots, black	Everyday tote bag, black
1764		Casual day dress		Parka / trench coat	Knee-high boots, black	Small clutch, black
1765		Little black dress			Knee-high boots, black	Everyday tote bag, black
1766		Little black dress			Knee-high boots, black	Small clutch, black
1767		Little black dress			Round pumps, black	Everyday tote bag, black
1768		Little black dress			Round pumps, black	Small clutch, black
1769		Little black dress			Wedges, tan	Everyday tote bag, tan

TROUSER/ PANT	SKIRT/ SHORTS/ DRESS	TOP	OUTERWEAR	SHOE	BAG
1770	Little black dress			Strappy heel, black	Everyday tote bag, black
1771	Little black dress			Strappy heel, black	Small clutch, black
1772	Little black dress			Ballet flats, black	Everyday tote bag, black
1773	Little black dress			Ballet flats, black	Small clutch, black
1774	Little black dress		Cardigan, black	Knee-high boots, black	Everyday tote bag, black
1775	Little black dress		Cardigan, black	Knee-high boots, black	Small clutch, black
1776	Little black dress		Cardigan, black	Round pumps, black	Everyday tote bag, black
1777	Little black dress		Cardigan, black	Round pumps, black	Small clutch, black
1778	Little black dress		Cardigan, black	Wedges, tan	Everyday tote bag, tan
1779	Little black dress		Cardigan, black	Strappy heel, black	Everyday tote bag, black
1780	Little black dress		Cardigan, black	Strappy heel, black	Small clutch, black
1781	Little black dress		Cardigan, black	Ballet flats, black	Everyday tote bag, black
1782	Little black dress		Cardigan, black	Ballet flats, black	Small clutch, black
1783	Little black dress		Blazer, stone	Knee-high boots, black	Everyday tote bag, black
1784	Little black dress		Blazer, stone	Knee-high boots, black	Small clutch, black

TROUSER/ PANT	SKIRT/ SHORTS/ DRESS	TOP	OUTERWEAR	SHOE	BAG
1785	Little black dress		Blazer, stone	Round pumps, black	Everyday tote bag, black
1786	Little black dress		Blazer, stone	Round pumps, black	Small clutch, black
1787	Little black dress		Blazer, stone	Wedges, tan	Everyday tote bag, tan
1788	Little black dress		Blazer, stone	Strappy heel, black	Everyday tote bag, black
1789	Little black dress		Blazer, stone	Strappy heel, black	Small clutch, black
1790	Little black dress		Blazer, stone	Ballet flats, black	Everyday tote bag, black
1791	Little black dress		Blazer, stone	Ballet flats, black	Small clutch, black
1792	Little black dress		Blazer, black	Knee-high boots, black	Everyday tote bag, black
1793	Little black dress		Blazer, black	Knee-high boots, black	Small clutch, black
1794	Little black dress		Blazer, black	Round pumps, black	Everyday tote bag, black
1795	Little black dress		Blazer, black	Round pumps, black	Small clutch, black
1796	Little black dress		Blazer, black	Wedges, tan	Everyday tote bag, tan
1797	Little black dress		Blazer, black	Strappy heel, black	Everyday tote bag, black
1798	Little black dress		Blazer, black	Strappy heel, black	Small clutch, black
1799	Little black dress		Blazer, black	Ballet flats, black	Everyday tote bag, black

	TROUSER/PANT	SKIRT/SHORTS/DRESS	TOP	OUTERWEAR	SHOE	BAG
1800		Little black dress		Blazer, black	Ballet flats, black	Small clutch, black
1801		Little black dress		Parka / trench coat	Knee-high boots, black	Everyday tote bag, black
1802		Little black dress		Parka / trench coat	Knee-high boots, black	Small clutch, black
1803		Little black dress		Parka / trench coat	Round pumps, black	Everyday tote bag, black
1804		Little black dress		Parka / trench coat	Round pumps, black	Small clutch, black
1805		Little black dress		Parka / trench coat	Wedges, tan	Everyday tote bag, tan
1806		Little black dress	Three-quarter sleeved top, black		Knee-high boots, black	Everyday tote bag, black
1807		Little black dress	Three-quarter sleeved top, black		Knee-high boots, black	Small clutch, black
1808		Little black dress	Three-quarter sleeved top, black		Round pumps, black	Everyday tote bag, black
1809		Little black dress	Three-quarter sleeved top, black		Round pumps, black	Small clutch, black
1810		Little black dress	Three-quarter sleeved top, black		Wedges, tan	Everyday tote bag, tan
1811		Little black dress	Three-quarter sleeved top, black		Strappy heel, black	Everyday tote bag, black
1812		Little black dress	Three-quarter sleeved top, black		Strappy heel, black	Small clutch, black
1813		Little black dress	Three-quarter sleeved top, black		Ballet flats, black	Everyday tote bag, black
1814		Little black dress	Three-quarter sleeved top, black		Ballet flats, black	Small clutch, black

	TROUSER/ PANT	SKIRT/ SHORTS/ DRESS	TOP	OUTERWEAR	SHOE	BAG
1815		Little black dress	Three-quarter sleeved top, black	Parka / trench coat	Knee-high boots, black	Everyday tote bag, black
1816		Little black dress	Three-quarter sleeved top, black	Parka / trench coat	Knee-high boots, black	Small clutch, black
1817		Little black dress	Three-quarter sleeved top, black	Parka / trench coat	Round pumps, black	Everyday tote bag, black
1818		Little black dress	Three-quarter sleeved top, black	Parka / trench coat	Round pumps, black	Small clutch, black
1819		Little black dress	Three-quarter sleeved top, black	Parka / trench coat	Wedges, tan	Everyday tote bag, tan
1820		Little black dress	Three-quarter sleeved top, black	Parka / trench coat	Ballet flats, black	Everyday tote bag, black
1821		Little black dress	Three-quarter sleeved top, black	Parka / trench coat	Ballet flats, black	Small clutch, black